CONVERSATIONS AND VERSIFICATIONS

ALSO BY MARVIN COHEN

The Self-Devoted Friend (1967) Rapp & Carroll (UK) and New Directions (USA); *Expanded 50th-Anniversary Edition* (2017) Tough Poets Press

Dialogues (1967) Turret Books

The Monday Rhetoric of the Love Club and Other Parables (1973) Rapp & Whiting (UK) and New Directions (USA)

Baseball the Beautiful: Decoding the Diamond (1974) Links Books; Second, expanded edition as *Baseball as Metaphysics* (2017) Tough Poets Press

Fables at Life's Expense (1975) Latitude Press

Others, Including Morstive Sternbump (1976) Bobbs-Merrill; *Expanded 40th-Anniversary Edition* (2016) Tough Poets Press

The Inconvenience of Living (1977) Urizen Books

How the Snake Emerged from the Bamboo Pole but Man Emerged from Both (1978) Oasis Books / Earthgrip Press

Aesthetics in Life and Art, Existence in Function and Essence and Whatever Else is Important Too (1982) Gull Books

How to Outthink a Wall: An Anthology (2016) Verbivoracious Press

Five Fictions (2018) Tough Poets Press

Inside the World: As Al Lehman (2018) Sagging Meniscus Press

Women, and Tom Gervasi (2018) Sagging Meniscus Press

Run Out of Prose (2018) Sagging Meniscus Press

Sadness Corrected: New Poems & Dialogues (2019) Sagging Meniscus Press

Life's Tumultuous Party: Reduced to its Essential Partycycles (2020) Sagging Meniscus Press

Plays on Words (2020) Tough Poets Press

CONVERSATIONS AND VERSIFICATIONS

Marvin Cohen

Edited by Colin Myers & Maggie Beale

Tough Poets Press
Arlington, Massachusetts

Copyright © 2021 by Marvin Cohen.

Front and back cover photos copyright © 2021 by Maggie Beale.

Preface copyright © 2021 by Colin Myers.

Afterword copyright © 2021 Deborah Sanderson & Peter Jackson, to whom many thanks for their friendship and support.

ISBN 978-0-578-81263-2

Tough Poets Press
Arlington, Massachusetts 02476
U.S.A.

www.toughpoets.com

To my wife, Candace Watt

CONTENTS

Foreword 9
Author's Non-Preface 11
Preface 11
From the Shoebox 15
Conversations from the Inbox 67
Versifications from the Inbox 155
Afterword 323

FOREWORD
by Candace Watt

Written on the day Marvin and I decided to get married.

Walking through the Brooklyn Botanic Gardens in mid-March:
Over there are crocuses, and here are snowdrops, dangling prettily;
But the trees are still bare—
Until you get up close.
Some buds are eighth-of-an-inch duck heads, sleek, flat;
Some are miniature asparagus tops;
Others fuzzy dark-blue caterpillars
Or velvety pussywillow buttons;
Still others wrapped flame-nuggets.
We ran out of words
When we thought of these little tips'
Holding
A sky full of blossoms.

[Candace Watt, 3/17/86: Marvin and I were married 5/22/86]

AUTHOR'S NON-PREFACE
by Marvin Cohen

I can't think of an Author's Preface, since the book's contents often seem like not only their own prefaces, but their own aftermaths.

PREFACE
by Colin Myers

From Shoebox to Inbox

The author James Sallis said Marvin Cohen's first book "*The Self-Devoted Friend* (1967) is a collection of short pieces [which] are variously narrative, dialogue, essay, epigram—some are surreal, some are pastiche and parody, some are reminiscent of Baudelaire's *Petits Poèmes en Prose*. Ellipsis is the predominant quality: the reader is asked to accept this material, this disparate substance strung together with associate devices . . . Parts are superbly comic [though it does not] afford the reader easy entrance . . . It deserves reading; there is, at least, nothing quite like it. Cohen is trying to explore the possibilities and expand the limits of the fictional form. For this, and for the large measure of success he achieves, attention is due him." [*New Worlds*, #181, April 1968]

Over fifty years later, there is still nothing quite like it, except, of course, Marvin's subsequent writings.

The first part of this book comes from Marvin Cohen's big shoebox of unpublished typescripts, mainly dating from the 1970s and 1980s. The rest comprises dialogues, monologues, sketches and verse selected from his recent emails to a number of friends.

Author's Absent Autobiography

When asked whether he ever considered writing an autobiography, Marvin emailed back: "i'd hate to write direct azutobiography because i need to fantasize, distort, exazggerate, extrapolate, & digress into mental & emotional meaznderings. the unnesessazry "z" letter comes a lot as you can notice, because of gnarled distotorted fingers from playinging years of soft-ball & getting my hands banged & knocked around into bony disfiguring, gnzarled." *[Email dated April 27, 2020]*

On Dialogues, Mini-Plays and Semi-Non Plays
Many of Marvin's "dialogues" can be read as internal monologues, showing "a mind trying to fix itself and experience in speech, to give voice to experience and time . . . The message, echoed in so many contemporary self-reflexive fictions, could result in a state of impotence and desperation . . . But the voice which animates these self-conscious and amused texts delights in its fictiveness, making itself a self-conscious artifice in which the mind's persona achieves a degree of abstraction that makes it read like an essay." [Charles Russell, *The Avant-Garde Today*, 1981]

A Note on the Verse
Marvin Cohen's style varies from the elegaic to didactic hip-hop (though he claims never to have heard of hip-hop or rap), with an emphasis on rhyme or punning. The content, in part, serves as an old man's diary, returning again and again to the nature of aging: loss of friends, virility, memory and mortality. Indeed, Marvin says: "I'm acting my age by writing about my age, obeying the advice to writers to write about what they know, or fear, or apprehend." His other musings are mainly on love and living, fidelity and rejection, evolution, nature and sport (expanding on his book *Baseball the Beautiful*) as well as writing about the process of writing itself.

A Note on the Words
Marvin Cohen's neologisms and portmanteau words are normally intended. When I emailed him that "I've been converting your typescript into a computer-friendly format. In doing this, I've noticed words that don't appear in my dictionaries nor are legitimately derived from existing words. Any chance of confirming your original (distant)

intentions? Here's a handful, with possible alternatives:

        debatedly   [could be: debatably?]
        flirtationality   [could be: flirting?]
        genuinity   [could be: genuineness?]
        gregaiety   [portmanteau: gregarious & gaiety?]
        slench   [portmanteau: slake & quench?]"

Marvin's reply was: "use debatably. use flirtionality. use genuinity. use gregaiety. use slench."

A Quick Read
If you don't have time to read all of this book then sampling just the titles of these dialogues and poems will be an insightful introduction to this humourous, sometimes brutal but gentle writer.

FROM THE SHOEBOX

A HOPEFUL SERMON

There's a false excitation going on in New York, driving spurious spikes of stimulation through people, like papers flung stirring by the wind's frisky broom.

Although the excitement is falsely stimulated, yet nevertheless a natural result may ensue, and real works may be produced, for you're the transformer of artifice into pure products. Thus a farmer may keep the electric bulb shining all night in his hen's artificial cage, resulting in the same eggs that would have been born by day. Good things may come about through dubious means,

Yes, and a poet may be struck to inspired frenzy and a rhapsody of lyric triumph, a welling out of imperishable verse, by the illusion love casts from a girl who by actual standard is undeserving of so twistedly lavish a dreamborne estimate and sustained artifice. But a heroic she-myth may have been created, by the incredible transformation. Contributing to the poor richness of our dreary world.

Let's contrive to make true things from the false ones. By no means should we scorn the good ends meanly arrived at. Our works shall vindicate any process, though responsibility attends each consequence in the path. Ill winds may be laden with the seeds of mildest bliss.

INDEBTEDNESS TO THE PAST: BUT NEVER TO BE PAID OFF

When I think of the past, it grips me with nostalgia.

It fires *me* with regret.

It whips me into despair.

It thrills me with remorse.

It quenches me with anger.

It impels me to fury.

It quiets me with contemplation.

It annoys me to think about it.
Why? What has it ever done to *you*?
Everything! It's all I am!
Oh. What do you owe it?
Me! Body and soul!
Can't you give it less?
Then how will my debt be discharged?
The past might give an amnesty, and *withdraw* its charge.
And, rid of the past, I'm supposed to be free?
You're quits with your *debt*; but you and your past resume: as equal partners, to a continuing journey, an unfinished adventure.
A joint venture? But where?
To the past that's yet to be.
Thus padding my debt further!
Forget the debt. You'll die, first.

WORLDLY ADVOCATE OUTPERSUADES THE WOULD-BE OTHERWORLDLY

First character: The otherworldly dream man.
Second character: The stay-at-home type, who likes it here.
Scene: Here.
Time: Now.
Place: (See "Scene.")
Costumes: Optional.
Theatre: Wherever people are.
Director: Open.
Price of Admission: Whatever falls short of incurring countercharges of profit-mongering, although expenses must be met.

Stage: Bare, except for above-mentioned characters.
Lighting: Between white and black.

I always like to dream of higher things.

I always like to dream of lower things.

Then who's on the right track, you or I?

I think between us, we've got the world made.

But what of things outside?

There *is* no outside. The world is as wide as there is. Once you reach the end of it, it stops. We're always confined within the world's wide boundaries. I can anticipate your argument. You're going to accuse me of the finite and narrow view of the old navigators in the age of exploration who expected that if they kept sailing on the salt brine they'd wind up falling off the flat end, boat and all, a fate equal to death. Then astronomers came along to prove that the world was not flat. But now *I*'ve come along, and do stoutly maintain that the world has edges. Don't blow astronomy into my ear, it's hot air. All I want is a woman with ass and tits, and to hell with all theories of the mythological "outside." I haven't settled the inside yet. There's more pleasure to be gotten, more joy to be tapped, here where our bodies lodge. We keep feeding ourselves. We get plastered on drink, like the heathens we are. We're busy arranging our comforts, We want to feel at home in the world. Home is where the heart is. But our hearts are only where our bodies are, even where there are dreams and memories. I'm sticking to this world. *You* go outside.

After hearing you, *I*'m staying here too.

Good. You weren't going any where any way.

No, I *thought* I was. But I'm not.

CHALLENGING ONE'S SUPERIOR, AND RELENTLESSLY BEING OVERCOME BY HIS ADVANTAGES, IN STUBBORN DEFIANCE AND STRENUOUS FAILURE AGAINST HIS HIGHLY BRED EASE

(Two characters: a pugnacious one, high-pitched; and an elegant, lax, condescending one. Continuous, but one-sided, rivalry between them.)

I'm asserting myself. Why aren't *you* as pugnacious?

I don't *have* to be.

What is your assurance due to, and your great pose of confidence?

Whereas you must *assert your* identity, *I inherited* mine.

Then you had a head start on me!

But it didn't *go* to my *head*: it was due to breeding.

(Competitively:) But there's nothing wrong with *my* breathing: my nostrils are perfectly clear, and force their way through to the outer air, with a terrific suction noise.

Is that cause for gloating?

What's *your* big boast, you grand thing? Do you dare oppose me?

But my mouth was gilded with a silver spoon, at birth.

(Competitively:) Well, *I* use a *knife and fork*: nothing wrong with *my* table manners!

Oh, don't put on airs.

I *will* put on heirs, as soon as I father them and leave them their legacy I'll earn through working good and hard.

What are you trying to *prove*?

That I'm a better man than you, *any* equal day.

Oh, Well I don't *have* to *try:* I am superior. *(Walks confidently away.)*

(Pugnacious one stares, startled. When other has left the stage, pugnacious one sags, dejected. And millions of inferiority worms climb over

his gloom. No blustering swagger will do for him now, that he's alone. He lost, feels lost, and has yet to lose some more. His only consolation is to nurse his envy. And play his Big Man role, once the next competitor arrives: whom he bolts up looking for, in an exaggerated stride.) (Preceding description must be conspicuously mimed, in gross, stylized effect.)

THE JOB INTERVIEW BY A PROSPECTIVE EMPLOYEE WITH THE PERSONNEL DIRECTOR GUARDING THE ORGANIZATION FIRMLY AGAINST ALL BUT QUALIFIED, RELIABLE, AND LUCKY APPLICANTS OF RESOURCEFUL TENACITY

(Characters: Personnel Director sitting behind desk; solicitous applicant, in the awkwardly assumed posture of confidence and poise, standing at trial.)

(Notes for atmosphere-direction: Moods go up and down in quick shifts in balances of power between the antagonist characters; often with inexplicable caprice. Nothing necessarily leads to the next stage. Abrupt changes of situation will occasion themselves without warning, careful preparation, or apparent reason. A lighthearted arbitrariness must be at all times ready to take charge during a constant emergency situation, The plot is notably unsound, unbased, void of foundation. That leaves the whimsical to support the displaced weight, with its spontaneous gracings of buoyancy to lift the play from flopping down in structural disaster. The director's guile must compensate for a craftless playwright. And the audience must be beguiled into gracious-hearted forbearance and the total unified suspension of its collective critical capacity. To exonerate the playwright, for his glaring faults and omission of a planned core central to the play's vacuous expanse of meaning, only courageous directors need apply. Others seek positions less tasking of their talents or risking of reputations-in-waiting.)

What are you here for?

To be interviewed for a job. I was to hand in my filled-out questionnaire form—listing my employment record, past experience, suitable references, current availability, and qualifications if any—to the personnel director, who would then question, test, and hire me, as he saw fit. Are you he?

That's me. Who else but I could be at my desk?

I request to be permitted to take the liberty of telling you what a grateful privilege it is that you personally—

—That's no flattering distinction for you: I interview everybody. Despite my glorified title, I'm only an inferior functionary here *myself*.

Oh. Well, may I have the honor of applying—

—Your application is being duly considered. We'll have to check your security risks, and other pertinent data. We'll let you know when the time comes. Go home and wait for us to call you. But don't depend on it. Better apply elsewhere as well. There might not be an opening at the present time. If this has been disappointing—if you had hoped to be hired on the spot—then accept our profound regrets. We're quite filled up, right now. All positions are closed. Perhaps if we find cause to fire one of our present help, you might be called to replace him. But currently all is satisfactory with our staff, and all departments and offices are accounted for. Doesn't leave much room for *you*, does it?

I had expected something more—

—You were wrong. My time is valuable. Will you please dismiss yourself? Temporarily your application will be filed inactively, till we find better use for your abilities— *(Abruptly:)* which are what?

I have typing skill at considerable speed with inaccuracies kept to a minimum; I know how to make up forms and reports; I take shorthand dictatorship—rather, dictation—as quickly as taped or delivered; I know how to file records and keep references well-tabulated to hand at the first accessibility; I'm an earnest, conscientious worker; I have leadership ability, but take orders without question; I can improvise an unprecedented problem through to its solved emergency; I can think quickly if needed, as well as recite by rote. Though I obey rules and regulations, I have inventive originality for special cases; the firm's profit is always uppermost in my mind for every decision I make or order I execute; I'm economic, efficient, and clear-thinking; I'm mathematically inclined, and have a head for figures; I have a temperamental aversion for disorder, and I'm prompt to dispatch all matters in the right channels; I have an ingrained respect for, and submission to, authority; I'm a go-ahead man, a take-charge man if necessary, avid for responsibility, keen for promotion, a potential executive, honest and loyal and hard-working, whose every thought is for the company. I'd be willing to work my way through the organization, and though keeping my subordinate place in keeping with my level or post, can swiftly climb to the top, displaying skills in the command of men for being unwilling to take inspirational initiative. And my life is devoted to business. I have a sound head for it.

All very impressive. But aren't you boasting?

No, these are my modest shortcomings.

That's even *more* impressive: *astoundingly* so. I suppose we can't turn down a man of your abilities: you'll have to be hired.

But all your positions are filled, you said.

We'll have to make room for you. We can't afford to lose you.

I'm honored to belong to your highly accredited company. What's my starting salary?

As befitting your capacities, high. You're now in a prestigious firm. Do well by us, and we'll do well by you. Rewards and bonuses will pad your nest. I congratulate you. *(Stands up and shakes new employee's hand; then sits down again. Refers briefly to typed paper:)* You may begin Monday, at nine sharp, report to the fourth floor, your supervisor will be—

—I quit!

Already?! What for? Personal reasons, family problems, poor health, the need to relocate?—why such a precipitant action? You may regret it. State your reason. I find you most abrupt, and insulting. You have no control over impulse. You would have been a poor risk. If you hadn't quit, we were just ready to fire you, the discharge papers were being typed in our secretarial pool, to give you terminal leave forever, without reimbursement. *(Sharply:)* You must *work* for your benefits, remember.

Will you reconsider? I regret my sudden explosion. It was totally out of character. I promise you a more earnest, and subdued, and sobered wiser, and contrite, employee. Punish me with a humble position: I hope to make amends.

We admire your spirit. *Everyone* slips up, from time to time; your personal failing will not jeopardize your official—

It was uncalled-for. I'm *much* more thorough than that. May I give you a trial demonstration of my worth? At full pay. But I promise results.

You're a fixture. We need you. Your value has an unlimited rating; once you harness your spontaneous outbursts.

I shall dearly fulfill my conditions for qualification. I'm your man. We've already been through so much.

Yes. I feel you're a *veteran* of the payroll.

Business is experience in life. It pays off.

[The above was read by Marvin Cohen and Wallace Shawn, at "The Poets at The Public," New York, December, 1978]

A FARCE OF TRIUMPH OVER OBEDIENCE, OF DOMINATION CAPTIVATING THE VANQUISHED, OF CONQUEST OVER SUBORDINATION, INEVITABLY OVERCOMING THE SLIGHTEST RESISTANCE

Do you know Robin?

No, but I hate him anyway.

On what grounds?, since you don't know him.

Because *you* like him.

Oh. It flatters me to be so highly regarded, that to protect your individuality you feel obliged to contradict me; If you *also* liked Robin, would your similarity to my point of view threaten to deprive your identity of its distinctiveness?

Yes. I feel protected when I'm disagreeing with you. I want to steel my boundary safe from being overlapped by your expansionist personality that would colonize my mind and subordinate it to *your* taste, *your* will, and *your* moods.

(With gleeful discovery:) Am I *that* aggressive? Not until encountering your fear have I realized it!

Yes, So it's my policy to dislike Robin, to counter *your* liking him.

How powerful I am, so sway you to such arbitrary opinions as a singular defense against my formidable strength! *(Preening himself:)* When did my vanity last receive such a boost?

Yes, you *do* bear watching. I'm not safe.

Nor are *you free,* when your mental preoccupation is to form contrary opinions to mine, rather than freely to determine your own! So automatic is it, in predicting what stand you'll have to make! Your sole function is a very restricted one: the defiance of me!

Your strength has limited me to such a weakness: that's how it goes.

So that should I decide to reverse my liking for Robin into a loathing for him, then it falls to you to switch sides accordingly, by your inevitable resistance to me, and it follows that you must adore him.

My duty. Our conflict must be preserved, and my dissent deliberately maintained. To avert the danger of my *becoming* you. You're so overwhelming, that should I relax, I'd be swept into your dominion by the force of your suction. I must parry, negate, and counter, your least thrust.

Which I'm not even aware of making! You are *really* defining me! I never felt so bold before!

Your exuberance would take over my weaker will and confiscate my self-determination. To be independent of you, and not be absorbed into your greater system, necessity requires an incessant *fight* on my part. It takes all the energy I can summon to be sufficiently relentless as to neutralize your devastating infiltration. I must doctor myself, to ward off infection. Your pervasive influence needs a constant administration of sterilizing, or your gain would sweep my will away and make me but an annex of *you!*

(*Joyously incredulous:*) I feel so mighty! What have you done to me!?

You will not rule me. I defy you. What season is this?

Spring.

Then, regardless of *what* season it is, I must opine that it's *autumn!*

In your given state of manic phobia that blindly must contradict me, how little heed you give, and disrespectful inconsequence, to *Reality*, reduced to irrelevant impotence by your unremitting warfare against me! You're obsessed! Reality is for moderate minds.

I'm too stubborn to listen to what you say!

On the contrary! You can listen to nothing else! All is pointless that doesn't nourish an active disagreement with me! You must contest my every word, and concede not even a nuance! You've imprisoned your fate into that of my solo antagonist! That's the most narrow specialization you can have! Your shrinking has compacted into one dimension! You're a tool of dissension, and gyrate not a single degree of flexible scope in liberty outways . . . You're my rigid nemesis. How stiffly you wait in stony bitterness against what I next might say!

Whatever it is—my answer, invariably, you can depend on it, is "No."

I'm not appealing to you—I'm only being what I am! *I* stand *my* ground!

A factor of my being undermined. I must hold on to what I have. And so I don't grant you even the right to be recognized, lest *I* be swamped!

You surrender your whole liberty, just to deny me my very existence, that imperils yours!

It's a state of emergency. Defense is my only hope. To me, you *must not* be valid. I must nullify your every move.

Your obsession has now become a threat to *me!* Your compulsive denial of everything I say has no longer that *flattering* ring. I want to stamp you out, and cut your opposition down. A crisis has sprung up between us!

(With grim automaticness:) I don't believe it!

I insist!

No!

(Reversing:) Oh. Then you win.

(Confused:) I win? No! I lose.

(Determined to agree:) All right: You lose.

Then I win!

All right: You win.

No! I've lost.

Of *course* you have!

My will won't break down: *No:* I've won.

You said it: You won.

(Imploring:) Believe me: I lost.

Then let me agree with you: All right, you lost.

(Breaking down:) Did I lose?

(Authoritatively:) Yes; you did.

(Marvelling:) You're masterful. I agree.

(Complacently triumphant:) I *knew* you'd come around to see my way, Oh, why were you such trouble?

My nature, it's so quarrelsome: I'm to blame.

(Maternally cajoling, lulling:) Shall we bury all bones of contention, like good little dogs?

We must, and subdue all strife.

Those bleached bones of contention. Are you properly brainwashed?

(Like an automaton, or loyal robot:) You *say* it: I *yes* it.

Of course. Need we go on?

No.

I *knew* you'd say that.

(In mime, the total subjection of the subjected man. He is dominated utterly. He dances a doglike, craven obedience. The other, supremely, is. He doesn't have to justify himself. The vanquished one minces actively, cowardly, on pointed toes. He dare not be still. He dances attention, the very parody of courtesy. It degenerates into a nimble ballet. The victor is quiet, and still. The other prances, with frenetic eagerness. Every gesture is that of neurotic submission. This becomes exaggerated, into a total caricature. It's clear, when the curtain comes down, that a farce has been acted. There must never have been one note of "realism.")

TED'S UNCONVINCING TALE

I

Ted loved to boast of his travels, to the envy of the stay-at-homes who listened begrudgingly to tales they themselves would have liked to be able to tell.

They clustered round him. After-dinner smoke kept the room's upper air as fluid as a transport system operated on the principle of vaporous particles of tobacco.

"On one of my recent excursions," Ted intoned, confident that his vocal tank had been refueled at the filling repair station with a guaranteed mileage of high-powered verbal wind, "I quite slipped off the edge of the world, just outside the boundary observed by every geographical map. Normal chart or compass now useless, I was forced to add another dimensional sense (improvised by this critical emergency) to my well-stocked arsenal of directional manoeuverability. The strain was such, that even I flinched."

He paused, gaining his point of emphasis. His audience was hooked, in a grim and breathless hush. Fumes from suspended cigarettes stuck to the static intersection where various intervals of rhythm met. The scene compelled Ted to continue.

"As you know, the earth abruptly drops off (like a waterfall cascade from a steep vertical mountain peak) at the end of its terrestrial territory. No explorer has dared to roam outside.

"My courage was a novelty without precedence. I was uniquely new to a zone spatially mythological, so virgin was it to the human rapacity of eyes or feet. The outer stratosphere, or the glacial arctic, or the accessible moon, were within child's play's distance, compared to where *I* had arrived (like a God who, being lost, had stumbled upon the momentous wilderness of an undiscoverable, but actual, universe).

"I surveyed what I could see, incredulous with incredulity. Here I was, where no man, beast, or mineral had ever set up a post of migratory location. I tell you, I was a*wed almost to deity*. Had lightning chosen that moment to strike its proverbial bolt, I would have dropped dead to the soul of my life. Even I was ill-equipped with rules of how to react. It would have staggered Einstein, disturbed Newton, and worked up Galileo; it would have uncynicized the foremost Russian or American space experts. It would have made an eyeless cat wink; and caused a bark to become a dog. It would have made butterflies chew on grass, and caused clouds to hang out advertising banners. It would have made horizons vertical, and chased the sun from its crows-nest to a noon Hades in the dungeon of midnight black. It would have frozen music to a sculptured plasticity dripping with words carved out of oil paint. It would have prosed over poetry (in a gloss of journalism), and created a nonobjective basis of abstraction into whose fount photography would surrender its entire visual empire of detailed realism. It would have made girls misconceive, and mothers grown heavy with the biological superimposition of an appendix of heavy ball-and-chain genitals hitherto only worn (at the fork of their pants) by the race of men. It would have—"

"Shut up!" an interruption shouted. "Don't exaggerate into hyperbole, if you wish to keep up our audience interest. Can't you tell us simply what you saw, what you found? It's a hard task to make believable the unbelievable, so don't squander the rhetorical devices or your ingenuity on the orgiastic dissipation of exclamation! Tell us, in your own simple language, what happened."

As if vindicated, the smoking began to pour out of pipes and cigarettes with a profanity of resumed traffic. Ted's hold on his audience was slipping.

II

The initiative had fallen out of his grip. In the midst of his intended greatest tale (showing to what private extreme travel may be brought), he had met with rebuke's stinging scorn; been chastized in mockery's torture den. How could he land on his feet again? The rest of the people in the room launched interflowing circles of murmur, slovenly commonplaces of conversation's middle-register of mediocrity. They discussed daily subjects at an ordinary level. Ted was appalled, this affront to the intelligent unravelling of his superiority derived from a consensus of rebellious envy and undisciplined impatience; plus a will to disbelieve. It was like a jury of minor angels reprimanding God for a technical misdemeanor and sentencing Him to a limbo where His communicative sermons would waste their sublime echoes unneeded by reverent ears of the devout initiates. (There was no demand for Revelation. The Gospel was gagged dumb.) This determined Ted on a comeback, to restore his prestige to its slightly toppled throne.

III

But alien voices were now ascendant. To prevail over them, and regain his lost floor without resorting to parliamentary stratagem,

Ted shouted clumsy beginnings of sentences drowned out by majority rudeness. The message he had been forestalled from making (like a parcel in postal delivery arrested in transit by a vehicular smash-up on a four-lane main route across the state line between rival metropolises) was now in its permanent stage of interruption. It was wedged in tight between obstacles.

Ted began again: "I insist! . . . I traveled to such a wonderful place, but you won't even listen. Put on your manners, you who never go anywhere. Travel to a mental wonderland in a bout of vicarious adventure, by needing once more this tale I've never managed to even have begun to begin the completion of which at its fully drawn-out length. It will edify, but not bore; enlighten, but not corrupt; entertain, undetoured by tedious and rambling digressions. Briefly, now, this in it: I voyaged outside of the earth, both by land and on sea (the only available routes, since there was an air strike) I landed in an element so unknown that even I haven't formally filed an invention claim on it.

"So you can excuse me that I can't label that mysterious 'X' by a given name or term; without which, it remains undefined, both by me and for you. Now I'm returned from my wanderings; I bear a tale, and have divulged it. I'm a hero of myth, whisked back upstairs to the sunshine of the contemporary, from the somber underworld of phantoms that float or cruise in circles of never-ending regret. (Yet what happened to me was magnificent, the most exalted realm of the supernatural to which mankind is never admitted.) And now I have a report to file. What are my findings?"

Cleverly, Ted paused with psychological timing. The silence was so cluttered with sound's loud absence, you could have heard a vacuum drop, so attentive were the auditors trained on Ted's train of unfolding thought. Spellbound by this brilliantly elliptical speaker, with his elusive evasions and veiled symbolisms cunningly concealed in a fabric of subterfugal ambiguity, the inhabitants of the room were open to enriching news about things remote from their habitual stay-at-home location; some exotic relief for the commonplace regularity of existences rendered uneventful by a mode so stationary that they went nowhere outside their normal ken.

Here was Ted, having returned from the one ultimate adventure that no soul had ever conceivably undergone; he personified that romantic cloud called "Strangeness"; his very person was a trophy and a testimonial to the "Unfamiliar" turned to sharp focus and accessible dominion by magic a weird act of conjuring. Mouths groped open; needs yearned for the impossible; the practical skepticism of experience was for once shut up, and restrained; aspirations toward the sublime, like unicorns on a leash, were set free, ready to rumble toward extraordinary vistas. The sunshine of hope drowned the "wisdom" of disillusionment. Vulnerable credulity, surprised by its release from captivity, blinked directly into a trinkling shine from apostles of heaven's dawn. Ted was on the spot. He was depended on, for the sustenance of souls in an ecstatic, though hesitant, ignition of vicariously genuine self-revelation.

IV

"There I was: I, born and formed from worldly substance, was in a 'place' totally alienated from the imperialistic sphere of influence at the outpost of the world's aggressive science. 'Truth' had never ventured so far; the barrier that penned in knowledge like that confining an angry bull, was being rammed to the verge of trembling by the urgent horns so phallically impotent with the restless urge of far meadows with curvaceous cows to be realized and raped. Expansion craved to leap, like muscles ready to spring their owner's species into a radical evolutionary mutation. Obsolete glands and outmoded organs were on the verge of . . .

"Oh, I don't know what happened! Memory's blank wall is topless and bottomless; I can't climb over, or crawl under, or soar sideways! Despite the enormity of where I was so fortunate to visit, recollection can only refer to the framework of *this* world; and by returning, I've automatically abdicated the majestic crown of an experience too sublime for words. I'm *among* you now; I'm back. Therefore, in terms of the here and now, it fails to be possible to salvage that rare grace of where I had voyaged to ... That which my journey faced, my back is to now. (My disappointment in a grief.) What I found at the time I uncovered this gem of the soul's sight, was found while I wore in that plane a different skin from this you see me in now, in this room that empirically we share at this solid moment. I'm not made of the same stuff as when I saw my miracle. And so, not even is memory's respite, in tiny dose, granted by the pitiless close-fistedness of gods too ungenerous to drop a trace of consolation. I came back, to tell you nothing. This is what I've been trying to say."

Ted's saga, made desperate in its wrung-out, highly-strung, but paralytic conclusion, was thus stranded like an endless end; as a fish (laboring out its breath on a beach with the tide receding and too much land between itself and survival, dry sand intervening in its need for the taste of salty but vanished deeps) opens its futile mouth, to sound out a roundless "O"—like a prophet into the cavern of unpopulated wind.

THE CURBING AND SATIETY OF AN ILL-MANNERED APPETITE BY A DEDICATED REFORMER'S GLUTTONOUS ZEAL FOR PROSECUTION TILL THE ACCUSED EXCESS MUST VOLUNTARILY CEASE AND THE ONE CORRECTED IS CONDEMNED BY PENALTY TO THE MORTIFICATION OF TOTAL PERSECUTION FOR HIS OWN SAKE OF REFORM AND IMPROVEMENT BY PAIN'S SCORCHING OUT OF SIN'S ROOT REMNANT

Let's go and eat some food.
What a gross appetite you have!
Is eating so great a crime, then?
In itself, no. When practiced by elegant people, no. When set about in a civilized fashion, no. But you! Your coarse delight carves the innocence out of it, and can gulp the wolf down from the center of a lettuce salad!

Even when you slurp lentil soup from a bowl, you do it as though you were committing a cannibal act with a furtive explicit flair for sin on the open plan, being caught red-handed at just what you're confessing with confidential exploitation of guilt being stripped of its palatable hypocrisy and exposed naked from the neck down!

What are you blaming me of?

Of eating without repentance.

But I do munch while on a *stool*, at times.

That won't do. And the vulgar table before you!

My table is so orderly, and diverse, and balanced, it's like the page in the book just before page one.

(Suspicious:) How do you mean?

(Simply:) The Table of Contents.

Oh. *(Pause. Resumes berating, as before:)* And your dishes are so indelicate! You devour animals before they're slaughtered, and then you slander their ghosts by eating up the gizzards of their memories without the slightest napkin of apology for soaking the filthy stains of drool that drip off your goozing chin. You're cruder than the animals you eat!—at least they have the courtesy to be placidly dead. But you're so all-consuming, that your carnival of disgust circles itself with endless vibrations on a theme of ugliness.

(Protesting:) I'm not all *that* obscene!

(Ignoring that:) You inspire the mildest spectator to puke uneaten food and vomit all the rest. So blatant is the beast you're transparent of, that your guts are strewn in an open fishbowl, and your creeping stomach is an open-air testimony of what's indigestible! You bite off what chewing can never relay to the organs of putrefaction! And not the thinnest toothpick do you dangle, as a token of redemption thereafter! Of all the foulness that enters you, your breath retains what's worst and returns it to our listening neighbor's nose. I *find* fault in you, as a casual feat of nature: you spare me from *seek*ing it.

(Resentful:) You *are* being *very* critical. I do *more* than *eat*, you know!

But the way you eat contaminates every other feature, and lends it its vice. Food has so coarsened you, that your whole life and machinery for living it is one odious meal whose every swallow is uniformly devoid of taste, deficient in refinement's prime vitamin, and nourishes only the onlooker's reciprocal appetite for disgust. You revolt me, from fart to fart, along every course in your life's one continual meal.

Oh. So what's endearing about me?

An *angel* could discover that. But *I'm* not blessed with so advanced a case of compassion.

That's true. All the mercy you're granting me, added end to end, wouldn't add up to the slightest bit of food, for me.

That's your single standard for evaluation: *food*. All other ideals are set at nought, like an alarm clock that never moves from the time it's bought from a silent effigy in a store!

I tick by food's power alone, winding me into circular sustenance?

Its craving and surfeit alone mean your matter! Your most assertive creation is a hearty belch, or a burbling burp. And your musical knowledge ends there.

(Defeatedly indignant:) Well! I'm quite *limited*, according to you!

What you *are* limited to, is virtually unlimited! Food channelizes your compensation for every other department! It crowds the whole throb of life into one monster of organic monopoly and puffin pigdom glandulating its rare strain of obesity!

You've convinced me: I'll diet!

(Jolted violently in surprise:) What!? My diatribe has won?

Of course! I can't go on in the vein you've blasted me for! Your eloquence has converted my instinct into your reasoning; dried out my hot saliva on restraint's blotting pad and the palate's mortification; tightened gluttony's belt; and installed slender moderation in the pompous belly's place. Your tongue's scalding game converts me to your persuasion, and my body's bulge reverts its conviction to your scolding's law. I concede, and your point is scored.

(Disappointed; let down, rather than victorious:) Oh. Have you another fault?

Yes. Start correcting my sloth: then treat my envy, and slim down my pride. I have an endless array, to challenge your versatile mastery.

Good! We can resume our relationship! Now let me edify you, and rectify what's aberrant. I have a strait stricture for the crooked!

I submit: But shouldn't we first briefly retire for a slight repast or snack?

No relapse! We've new roads to mend, and Fault's awful blunders to smooth down. The first learning is host to a *score*. Eating's the least of you. One thing is purged; but gigantic More is in store. That norm is still far to which your reform can aspire, till reduced to nothing but what *I* might admire, and not grudge you for.

Be strict.

First tortured by austerity, then punished into severity: I'll make you *me*, yet.

Then will your plaguing stop?

Then *you* must start, on me.

Good. Have you sins, piled up?

I'll take all yours as you relinquish them. What you're cured of, *I* confiscate. Then it's *your* turn, me to convert.

What torment, is this zeal for reform!

Yes, the sharpest pleasure is pain, by puritanical degree.

Whose pain?

It doesn't matter.

And what gain?

The least food, on the starving platter.

Is that good?

Converted Bad is all the Good I know. Let's flagellate gluttony. And glutton on our flagellation. A moral cycle is delight's restoration of balance. Have you stopped eating?

I have.

Then even your deprivation must show etiquette!

It does: I abstain with all the mannered deportment of grace.

Good. Sins must be checked, with daily reprimand for regulated abuse, even when uncommitted or not duly considered yet. Bring Envy in, Pride, and Sloth. My correction will be stern, in each case, consecutive and in general. Nothing punishable may escape, What you softly allow is by steel's band unlearned. What's too rooted, must be gleefully burned. Virtue is in Vice's stead, and is solidly earned! And learning is only stamped by *pain*'s sullen ring.

That's the law you bind me to?

Yes, I'll grind it in. Pain will be no more hated. Pleasure's the fiend we must eradicate.

(Starting to supplicate, in posture of genuflection:) What must I placate?

(Lordly in magnificence:) Me. Your lord.

(Cringingly:) I cower.

(Mock-tenderly:) My flower!

(Weakly appealing, submissive:) Be easy, please?

No. All Good is by *hard*ness won, I'm afraid.

Oh. Pity me.

Then mercy would be your enemy. Bend your character to my decree. Alter all your will, to my leniency. Breathe brokenly by the permission you're given, and not by your daring to. Your least ray of sight is a dark debt to my light. Authority will treat; but you cannot take.

(Virtually prostrate:) My life is at your feet.

(Cruelly magnificent:) Good. I take my stand on that; and arch your spine down.

Will you rescue me, or am I bereft?

Your determination is not done yet. Let me think.

Is *wiping me out* to your pleasure?

You were very stout. Let your lean preparation come.

(Darkness, and then brilliant illumination. The total subjecting of one being to another. The scene pauses as a vivid silent tableau of mime. The finality sinks in. The curtain, too intimidated to fall, is released, to separate the audience from its terror. But the echo has been engraved, by the lingered suspension of the scene's contrasting shapes, one supreme and standing, the other fallen and wiped into the stage's horizontal disgrace. This scene must have a striking effect, until the very curtain, so that following the curtain each memory is bruised with it. The spotlights must be very harsh, as starkness should obliterate mercy; and mercy's softening moderation must be relentlessly restrained. Cruelty is the note, struck so emphatically that it remains. The irrevocable is unmuted, hence the detailed lighting.)

KEEPING LAW AND ODOR IN A BIG CITY

(Disgusted:) Did you smell him?

It offends me. Even his *dirt* was unclean.

Let's suggest that he bathe.

That's right. And also that he should take a bath.

Good. That's a *double* cleaning protection.

For we've two noses he should rub the insult away from.

And scrub and wash, till the odor sails away.

Soap, hot water, and an ivory bathtub.

I can just *feel* him sitting in it.

And the transparent water blacken instantly.

While he, at the same rate, would whiten sparkingly.

What a clear solution: Let's inform him. *(They run offstage after the maloderant. In a minute they return, walking with sagging dejection.)*

It's no use. We can't get close enough for him to hear what we shout, for his stink is powerful at long range.

The wind was blowing from his side to our side. We should have approached him the other way.

I'm not a wind expert. Let's mail him a letter.

But he wouldn't get it till *tomorrow:* that would have given the smell time to intensify, expend, increase—and even multiply, considering the vermin and other microscopic creatures, lice and the like, that have been forming warm domestic hearthholds in his stink's central nest. Let's telegram our advice that he bathe!

(Searching pockets and examining wallet:) It's too expensive for me.

I'm broke too. It looks desperate. The longer we talk and delay—well, his smell sure isn't diminishing.

No . . . Is he still in sight?

(Peering afar offstage:) I can't *see* him. But I can tell his *direction*.

(Look of disgust:) So can *I!* Well, we know he's that *(Indicating:)* way.

And that he's alone.

But it's the center of the city's shopping district! At the prime business time, the rush-hour for congestion!

No matter: you can bet the area is evacuated, thanks to him.

Thoughtful of people to give him room.

Yes, the city is renowned for its courtesy.

In a way, he *has* cleaned!

(Puzzled:) What do you mean?

He's cleaned a crowded part of town, of its crowd.

That's no substitute for the real thing! Everyone knows that cleanliness is *internal*.

[*The above was performed at the Arts Festival, Cambridge, Mass., May 1968*]

GUILT SELF-ACCUSED, OR GUILT BY SOMEONE'S POINTED FINGER. THE INSIDE-OUTSIDE TWOFOLD OPERATION OF GUILT

I just passed a policeman!

Good for you. What were you guiltless of?

Oh, all sorts of things. Mere mention of them would give me a criminal complex.

Then omit the catalogue of the crimes you didn't do. That way, your guilt won't be so apparent.

Still, passing a policeman must have meant *some*thing.

But you're innocent! It was only an accident you passed him.

Perhaps there was some ulterior design.

Unlikely. Your paranoia is accusing you, with no imaginable justification. What's weighed down your conscience, in a detriment of self-prejudice? Why does remorse plague you? Have you an unconfessed sin, lurking at an irritable nerve center? You ought to purge yourself in a bath of bubbling virtue, to wash clean your skin from the soul's lice of evil. Morality is old-fashioned. Why should it afflict such a modern guy as you? For discipline, I prescribe that you walk by a policeman with literally no semblance of guilt. Dare him to suspect you! Affect an ornate display of innocence. To prove your virtue, con him into not arresting you. Use all your tricks, to protect your right to not feel guilty. *He*'s just a dumb officer of the law. But you, you're a sophisticated expatriate of the Garden of Original Sin. So defy him. For what have you done? Legally nothing, and illegally nothing. Make sure you furnish this proof. Present your fullest credentials. That ought to show him!

But why make a point of it? Being conspicuous would incur his suspicion.

Because you're a man of principle! You make a public issue of your private innocence!

That convinces me. I'm off. If I return, you'll know how credible my innocence is. If not—well, I'll try to deserve my punishment.

I'm glad to see that you take ethics personally. If left high and dry in the abstract, it merely collects dust. "Right and wrong" require more martyrs of your calibre. For you introduce the *human* element. Now go off, and be sure to challenge a policeman to get the goods on you, who've practiced all the sleight-of-hand and petty deceits worthy of a professional lifetime of innocence. Why, to be arrested, you'll have to be framed! Let him know exactly how you stand. You're an untouchable citizen.

Yes, my guilt bristles to the defensive, till I'm exposed. Already, I'm proven innocent.

Then go, and air your righteous purity, the audacity you've earned by having abstained from every conceivable crime!

Then should I furnish him with a list?

Of the crimes you've neglected to commit?

Yes. Or should I omit such ostentation?

No, let *him* figure it out. He's paid to be acute.

Who? The cop?

Sure. You're not scared, are you?

Me? Why should I be?

Consult your conscience. Only you can judge.

(Thinks introspectively. Decides:) I'd rather let the cop do it. And take me off the spot.

Coward!

Ah, hell. The scruples of the self-accused would cripple my easy-going style. A guy like me needs revenge. I can't examine every petty fault. Life needs leeway, like a golf course. So, I'm going to hide out in the open. Then, I'll *never* be detected.

You've just confessed.

Yeah? Well don't reveal it. Unless you suggest *murder*, as a likely crime.

Me? I never interfere.

Good. Wait here. I'll come back, absolved. Then, we'll see how spotless *you* are. You moral hypocrite! *(Goes off. Leaves other standing, immobile. A curtain decides to drop.)*

MATTERS GRAVELY ELEMENTAL, UNDER SOLEMN DISCUSSION

Why is water so colorless and odorless?

Because it's wet through and through.

Why is it so soft and weak?

Because it hasn't become ice yet.

Why is it not a vapor?

Because it's still in its fluid state.

Is rotten meat still meat?

Yes, but rotten: append it with that adjective, "rotten."

Is a corpse a person?

No, only a former person.

Why only that?

It's no longer social. It's so pale, it's *beyond* the pale. Social give-and-take, communal intercourse, it's now become unfitted for. Its personality and identity, its very character and soul, are no longer there. It's entitled no longer to be considered a person. It's a "Was," that's all.

Is a car that's in a junk-heap, all gutted out and disrobed of motor, tires, wheels, windows, cushions, accelerators, and other typical "traits"—lying all weather-beaten in the junkyard, infinitely beyond use, devoid even of scrap value—is that car a car, yet?

No, because it's seen better days. It's only a car's cadaver; and is to the former car it was, what a person's corpse is to the person no longer "there."

Oh. Mortality is a grim issue.

Were it not for mortality, graveyards would be empty, cemeteries vacant, and burial grounds a mere theatrical hoax. Mortality fully enriches the past. It deepens history, and fertilizes its rich complexity. Mortality is of grave significance, to us who yet live.

It sure is. But I despise it, when it applies to me.

That's a natural attitude to take. It's understandable: even commonly so.

Well, I'm alive. For this durational while. I'm "me," still here.

THE USE OF PRAISE AS A SOCIAL BRIDGE TOWARD RAPPORT

(Characters: Two men who are dressed and look alike.)

How can you recognize me?

By your smell. What else?

But isn't my face more noticeable?

Only visually. But it can't compete with your stink.

That's an uncharitable estimate.

I'm not in this insulting-business for charity.

What are you in it for?

To extract the truth from its unpleasant surroundings.

What unpleasant surroundings?

You! Your stink is your most flattering fact, whether it emanates from your armpit, or between your balls, or from your vegetating mouth, or from the place where you bruise a chair in sitting down. The reason I don't wear a gas mask in your presence is that at least smelling you distracts from your more odious details that serve as the environmental setting for your putrefying odors. The more it's contemplated, the more reekingly unpleasant is "You" in your totality of unholies: like the wrong sounds that your mouth deems righteous to declare; the misfeatured appearance in your countenance; your ill-assorted emotional makeup, from a barrel of upside-downdimdumbheadedness; the unethical vileness of your morals; the ungainly asymmetry of your revoltingly mismatched knees and elbows; the deeply full-loaded-and-packed-solid-density of your stunning intellectual void; the lightheaded vacuum in your ponderously dead-weight mind; the ungraceful consistency of your unrelieved opacity; your stunted retardedness abortively precocious; your insane inanity and inane insanity; the rapid but vapid nothingness so essential to everything about you; your lacking of what's good and your abundantly having of what ideally should be lacked; your ripely decadent prematurity in its readiest obsolescence of prime; your glandular secretions clad as grand secrets; and your other imperfections.

What other imperfections?

The ones I didn't mention.

Oh. Thanks for not mentioning them.

Well, they were *indirectly* mentioned, for I included them, as an etcetera.

A *what*?

An additionally plus.

Additionally plus? But that's positive! I thought you were compiling a *negative* list of me.

Yes, but I'm so *positive* about your being so excessively negative, that the mere mention of it comes out as seeming enthusiasm. In reality, I scorn you to a fault.

To *a* fault? Didn't you imply that I had *many*?
Yes, but they're all wrapped up in one.
That's tidy! What *is* this compact unitary combination?
You! You're well-integrated.
But is the external core of my surface interior, at heart, truly vile?
Yes, my verbal insults pale impotently by comparison. What you *really* are outdoes my *worst* description of it.
Does even your *exaggeration* fall short of it?
By far.
Well, if my reality is more extreme than your words, I can putrefy *without* your commentary.
Are you inviting me to shut up?
Yes, what you say is outdone by what I am.
You render me absolutely speechless.
When all is said and done, I'm left with what I am.
Which can neither be unsaid, nor undone.
Then let's contemplate the monument. Whether agreeable or not, the *real* is monumentally itself.
Yes, and most unfortunately, for *your* case.
Your value-judgements are unwelcome. They screen the fact.
Yet the porous screen permits the *odors* to escape.
Reality is inescapable. I'm locked into what I am.
Yes, and even the *key* can't gain admittance. Are you sorry to be what you are?
It's unavoidable.
I know. Identity is hard to change, when tied in with existence.
Still, I live.
Yes, it's the limit of the consolations you're permitted. But surely living

can't be satisfactory, when *you're* doing it!?

Well, it's the best I can muster, and the only thing possible for me.

Yes; in your case, only the *impossible* would have helped.

Helped to what?

To cure you.

Cure me? Of what?

Of being only you. Such a handicap, you labor under!

There's no *labor* involved; I find it easy!

Ah, now *nature* is assisting you as your criminal collaborator! And it's become a habit.

In that revolting?

It doesn't comfort me.

Are *you* so great, that you can criticize me with impunity?

There's one thing in my favor.

What?

That I'm not you: no-one is.

But is that a *positive* virtue?

It's a real excuse to boast, not being the worst.

Then you can't be very ambitious.

No, but at least you've defined my *minimum* ambition. Anything over that mark is a gain, by rule with that measure.

So you vault over me?

Yes, and leave you scattered low in the dust.

Scattered? How many pieces am I assembled with?

As many as may make up the total of *you*, by becoming your components.

So I'm composed?

Into a composition.

You quite discompose me.

And your decomposition is a stinker!

Do I decompose? Then what's left of my *former* self?

Only you, as its latter version.

I have an aversion to being a mere version.

Why?

Well, your version, adversely, is not verse; you're too prose-aic.

I don't inspire poetry?

But you do: the satirical kind.

Why *that* genre?

Satire finds you an easy target to hit. You *lend* yourself to criticism.

Well, *return* me, when you've finished borrowing me.

Oh sure. You always snap back into your original shape. You're elastically rigid, in that way. You revert to form.

Oh. Is that complimentary?

Yes. I've been paying you great tribute.

Thanks. At no sacrifice to the truth?

No, the truth has been very cooperative. Perhaps a little too lenient: cheating by conceding some minor trifles in its malleable flexibility.

You've been stretching it?

Slightly. But it snaps back, and elastically assumes your final rigid form.

I'm not a corpse *yet:* don't flatten me out *that* much.

No, the stiffness isn't so advanced.

Specifically, can you single out what I am?

It's not been determined. I've only been tearing you to pieces, all this time.

Analytically, or by the operation of synthesis?

I'm not certain. But you *are* whole.

How so? (You *do* pick holes in me, in your fault-finding crusade.)

By being a hole. No more, only that. Unconditional, in fact. The surrounding substance is immaterial. Even your *environment* doesn't weigh in to matter.

Oh. You make me out to be flimsily insubstantial. Is that the impression I've been giving off, in spite of myself?

That's the *un*impressiveness, *because* of yourself.

Oh. Is there any attenuating factor, a silver-lined loophole in this densely hopeless negative fabric of grimly uniform threads?

No, finally. No redemption, at all.

Am I then lost?

Utterly and solely, a *lost* soul.

So I am lost? Well, by the process of elimination, that locates me as being found.

Confound it! *Explain* that capricious paradox you've just made.

Don't be irritably peeved. Your tone is impatient.

How is your state of being lost an indicator of how you may be found?

By the process of elimination. The secret is not to search for me where I'm *not* lost. This eliminates so many locations, that it directs the seeker to the place where I'm really found.

Oh. What a discovery!

Yes. It's the *found*ation of my whole being, as a spatial entity.

And what are you in *time*?

Time confirms me what I *spatially* am.

Then you stretch out into every universal dimension?

Yes, it's necessary, if I'm to expand.

But why don't you *contract*?

It's not in the *contract* I signed on the living dotted line.

Oh. So who are you?

Plainly, it's not *you, whoever* I am.

Are you sure?

Yes. Just to *look* at us is to tell us apart.

What distinguishes us in our separateness?

The fact that you're distinguished, and I'm not.

So you don't compare favorably?

No, the contrast is all in your favor.

Good. My relative superiority is established.

Due to my absolute *in*feriority.

Well, so there *is* a difference.

Yes. If two people are both alive, that doesn't make them equal.

No. Quality counts.

Yes, and your quality is the greater.

You're too low for me to waste time with.

Is that our cue to part?

It's our *part*ial cue to part. With that ex-*cue*-se, let's be partners to a parting.

Each separately to go his own way?

Yes, do you jointly agree?

I *join* you in that.

Good. Let's go.

(Side by side, in unison, they march off together, to one of the stage-wings, keeping equal step, and appearing twin-ly like two of a kind.)

A CHANNEL CROSSING

Now that this is England I'm in, I've decided to go to France.

What mode of transport will implement such an eastward decision?

I'm going by ferry.

How primitive! It's obvious that I must wish you "bon voyage."

I'm going to visit a big museum that never strays from its prominent river location.

How traditional of it to remain so steadfast and loyal to the place of its birth! On such intimate terms it must be with its own roots!

(Whispers:) Shh—not so loud. *(Aloud in normal stage voice:)* And some of its pictures and statuary are even older than itself!

The place seems to be *teeming* with senility. Won't your visit place your reputation in a certain danger?

Oh, *too much* prudence is negative altogether. I might as well go. Have you any friends or acquaintances in the big France city that I might phone or call on, or in some way meet?

No, but tell me, will your ferry cross the channel by *day*?

Yes, I leave in the morning.

How convenient, for I *do* know a certain fish that's usually at home bobbing up and down, to whom you might say hello in passing.

But is he on my route? I don't intend to tell the ferry's captain to deviate off course.

Oh, you won't be going out of your way. My fish friend haunts ferry routes as a matter of course, and is so friendly to daytime passengers that the sun licks the waves up higher to provide the occasion with a cake of genial froth.

I thought the churning *engine wheels* do that!

A boat is too busy *moving* to be concerned with artistic foam effects. So *do*, in passing, tell my fish hello, convey both my regards and my intention to come by myself in the near future so that we may have our little reunion.

I'm burning with curiosity: is your fish friend a *man* or a *woman*?

I never really *could* fathom its gender. Perhaps it's one of those sexless neuters that the pyschopathology textbooks occasionally complain about.

Really, I *don't* want to create a scandal . . .

Not very likely: don't lean too far over the railing or the crew on deck might suspect something fishy.

One more question: is the fish *English* or *French*?

I think it observes the boundaries of international neutrality . . . in the *nautical* sense, of course. *(Slight pause:)* Why do you ask?

Oh, just to make conversation.

That's so polite, it borders on rudeness.

Borders how?—in the nautical sense?

No, in the naughty sense.

Be sensible, or it goes for nought.

JUST BACK FROM A TRIP. BEARING A MENTAL CONTINUITY, BUT LEAVING THE COUNTRY BACK THERE

I've just blown in like the wind from a big trip.

Then where's your luggage, such as a suitcase?

I already brought it home, before being here.

That accounts for your not having it with you?

Yes, but meanwhile my big trip is still echoing like a reverberator in the recent memory department of my extensively recollecting head.

That's *mental* luggage.

But I carry it lightly. It keeps the trip going. I'm still on it.

But *physically* you're back?
In my metaphorical flesh, I am.
That's quite a trip. It follows you around.
Yes, but the country stays *there*.
Which country?
The one I took my trip in.
Oh, *that*. It would have never fitted.
In what?
In your luggage, suitcase, baggage.
That's just as well.
Why?
I didn't go there to *steal*, but just to look.
Looking leaves the things there, but stealing takes them away?
Yes. Observation is not theft.
Then you're internationally legal?
Not only that, my arms don't ache. What a heavy country it would have been to cart back!
Then it must have been mountainous.
No, it was mainly coastal. But those hotels and ships weighed plenty!
Yes. Looking is light. But lifting isn't.
But from my traveling I brought back *token trophies*.
Representative souvenirs, but not the whole country itself?
Right. I lifted lightly, with legal purchase.
So you've returned unaccompanied by guilt?
No guilt. But a bulging memory burden, carried lightly, instead.
Where?
My head. The usual storage place, active file cabinet, the portfolio of

personal documents.

That's in good safekeeping. The head. Transformer of brute stuff, solid substance, hard matter, actual material outside of yourself, into a nice private reference library, catalogue and all. Empirical, concrete data. To consult, at your leisure.

So conveniently handy! Evidence of the past. Proof of me having been.

But you still are.

My active library keeps on requisitioning, up to date. It's not a dead museum. It gives me my trip back. It restores, bodily, that country. I'm in it, on winged feet.

But you're here as well: you're back, too.

My recent traveling world fits well in the world I've come home to. The brain is an international negotiator. It's a smooth, influential travel agent. It's a space broker, linking times apart at a second's unity. It's packed my broadening travel to the ease of my return, at the closest consultation. Separate places, separate times, are joined to the brim of concord, each preserved and enhanced, in the all-altering Whole.

Your brain?

Where boundaries overlap, and sequence undergoes simultaneity. My little box. My magic.

THE SEA'S LOVER, FLOWING ON REACTIONARY CURRENTS, BACK TO THE CHEMICO-MYSTIC SOURCE OF EVERYTHING, ESPECIALLY LIFE, THE SEA'S FINEST CREATION OF THIRSTY DEPENDENCY, OF WHICH ADDICTION TO WHISKY IS ONLY ONE HOMELY SYMBOL OF LIFE'S WET COURSE IN THE TORRENTS AND FLUENT SPREADINGS OF PROGRESS ABOARD LAND

(Characters: Two men. The first speaker likes water.)

Why is the shore so near the ocean?

It's not—it's near the lake.

Even so—the *principle* is the same.

You and your principles—do they ever hold water?

And why must a bank be close to a river?

To float its liquid stock assets.

Stop being merely monetary. I'm talking about bodies of water.

A man or a woman is also a body of water.

Why?

Their body is full of inside water.

You mean blood-water, milk, beer, and orange juice?

Stop categorizing. It isn't polite.

But I only delivered a small *catalogue*.

On soggy, soaked, dripping paper.

Oh, dry off!

You're the one who showers forth. Stop spewing drench on me.

Sorry. I was only driveling.

I got caught in the splash.

Here's a rag *(Handing one over)*. Wipe yourself.

That won't make *you* dry.

Your cracks merely wash over me. But I emerge unscathed.

With a friendly little wave.

And why is a pond or a lake divided into waves?

To break up the monotony.

I never knew aesthetics left the land.

It *frequently* wades in the sea. Look at shells: they're full of beauty.

What *gave* them beauty?

Instinct.

I never knew instinct had such good taste.

Haven't you heard of instinctive taste?

Yes, but who cultivated it?

Farmers and teachers.

You talk like a hose.

I'm only a sprinkler for suburban lawns.

I *roar*, like an ocean main . . .

All you need is a fresh bath. To rub off the salt spots and the clinging seaweed.

Stop raining advice. Or I'll pour out my wrath on you.

I'll duck behind my open umbrella, and watch the drops rub off the umbrella's duck-back, for protective safety and defensive armament.

My sunny cloud won't threaten you. But why do coastlines border on seas?

For the sake of maritime tradition.

Why is a beach always so close to the water?

For the convenience of the swimmers who go too far out. Life mustn't be made too strenuous for the lifeguards. Rescues must haul the rescued onto land. That's called "dragging them back." Look at any geography map: it's full of water. Yet people are land-dwellers. Sand and rocks are near the water. The green is further in. Natural national boundaries are often determined by water. America is a country that ends where the Atlantic begins. Lately, it's *also* ended where the Pacific begins. Those are *natural* limitations. Where would geography be without them?

In the sea. Where the early evolutionary fish are still to be seen.

And captured too, for our diet. But I can't chart your tides: are you ebbing, or flowing?

I'm sitting right here, talking with you.

I thought we were standing.

We're sitting on our shoes: that proves me right.

We're standing *in* them. Is your head where your feet belong?

My head is all at sea.

Has it a compass to navigate by, and an astrological steering wheel for divine guidance?

Only my water-logged *brain* is used for that.

Where does it get its power? By sponging tears from your eyes?

I don't weep. I laugh instead.

But do you salivate when hungry?

Yes, it's a pre-appetizer sauce.

And are you one of those who urinate?

Yes, I suppose I fit that type.

Can't contain yourself?

Never *was* taught the discipline. But I only let go a few times a day.

Is your character devoid of restraint?

It's not *constantly* leaking from a source of the lack of will-power.

What happens to your bladder?

It varies between full and empty.

Are you sure you're quite graduated from the animal?

My *words* betray such a notion. Or have I only pumped a boast full?

Why don't you become a wheel or ale?

What did you say?

I meant an eel or whale. My tongue slipped.

Well, stick your tongue back in, and listen as I answer. Yes, I'd like to be a whale, *or* an eel. They're both very healthy creatures.

Is *health* the sum of all value to you?

You mean I should value sickness as well?

You avoid damp weather? You keep your feet dry?

I even dodge a drizzle, and run away from any fog.

Why not be a *frog:* at home both on land *and* sea, and hoarsely proclaiming his devotion to both.

Sounds like a croak, to me.

He's not creaking *to you:* he's croaking to a female frog,

For the mating business?

Eggs, and all that stuff. Messy, slimy, the primeval ooze. Like sap in the tree.

Did I ask for a biology lesson?

No, but you learned one anyway.

Very amphibious business.

You mean ambiguous?

Yes. *(Suddenly:)* I would like liquid refreshment.

Beer, wine, or whisky?

The quick route to drunkenness.

Why so fast? What's your hurry?

I've been sober so long, it's drying my bones. My throat has dust-parchments.

It's parched dusty?

Why correct me?

Just to get the script straight.

Script!?—*What* nondescript?

Here's whisky. *(Pouring from bottle to one glass handed to other, to another glass for self, Puts bottle away.)* Are you drunk yet?

I haven't started.

Are you retarded?

No, I'm slow to return.

What are you returning to?

To the sea before it was invaded by land. The sea that roars. At heart, I'm a sailor.

Have you ever been a boat passenger?

Yes, I was shipped from one continent to another for a tourist fee. I saw empty horizons.

Is the globe round?

Yes. But why doesn't the water keep slipping off?

There are docks, dikes, locks, and canals, to prevent that unnatural waterfall. Basins neatly keep the water straight. That's why "sea level" is a safe thing to say.

But what if floods don't give a *dam* for restrictions? Like fountains that spout at will, or high tides that come crushing in?

You sound wild. Can't you curb those images?

Do you advocate the *taming* of water?

Yes. Why drown dangerously?

You feel safer on earth?

It's terrain I can trust.
Old soil, and good dust.

I could wash your words away.
Give me lake, sea, or bay.

Our tastes oppose. I prefer land.

We're on your home ground *now*. Then, I'm your guest.

Your glass is done. I pour you more?

To be a host, you ought to. *(Gets glass refilled by other.)*

(Observing other:) The drink is taking effect. Your thoughts are leaving the land. They're perched on the deep sea.

Like the nautical diving birds. My Soul is on the blue, the green, the grey, the multi-colored sea. That always tumultuously moves, even in serenity.

It *is* known to flow. One of water's regular properties. Is that where your mind is floating?

I'm drifted. I'm being carried. Along a swift stream. On a river's narrow course, that twists through every overgrown banksides on devious currents. Out to the far and ample sea.

And *you*'re being drenched. Internally, with whisky.

The ripples toss me to and fro. The sea is hypnotic. I obey. And melt from my solid state. And pose to a liquid identity. I'm buoyed very far. I love ocean bodies. And the faucet tap.

The latter, drop by drop?

The former by the gallon. The sea bed is where I long to drop this mortal anchor, as my snug port.

Your swoon is bubbling from the deep. The froth is foaming through your ideas. Your weight is no longer land's. You *are* the sea. And in its element, as a wet entry, you're newly swept.

Better there. Land's solidity is tragic. Sorrow is *meant* to be drowned. *(Takes another sip of whisky.)* Light loves refraction. I'm borne in currents that ripple time's waves. Displaced, but imperishable. Replenishing, and immortal. Renewable, in the constancy of truth, whose varieties are all theme-bound. My harbor should be always afloat, tossing about. Or under, stripped of life. My love is sinkable. Yet is hurled by tides on the bouncing horizons. Serenity's a container that motion will fill. Follow the sea.

You're its vessel. Or it's yours. Your nostalgic inversion, relapse, regression, or visionary retrospect, to the humble fish state just past evolution's dawn. Do you want to unDarwin our whole progress? Hasn't man risen nicely from the wash?

I worship on old deity. It crumbles into foam. It runs through my grasping fingers—bunched into a fist, that porously sieves the running liquid through, in trails like insects, I retrogress, in this holy pursuit. I trail Man back to his origin. In the watery wake. The source gets my return. In that, I advance. I'm the backwards Darwin. You might call me all wet. Yet never was I sounder. Water has a rightness. Let me plant my original germ there.

The seed of fluency?

The fluid life that ventured on land with its own return ticket. The sun's sole love, bearing the opposite sex. Great air's sweet alter-ego. And the land's salty twin.

Are those the sea's forebears?

No, its living relations. It's a family of independent parts. But so joined, that here harmony centers inward and outward from these vital parts. Eliminate the sea, and nothing remains. A standard that *art* would do well to emulate.

Then is nature a sailor man?

Bandying his sea legs about. Ah, the swagger of him. The waves are the lesson. And far inland, they penetrate.

They touch you more then me.

My destiny is softer. It vies with the wet magic in me, from whisky, one of water's sublime creatures. *(Takes another sip.)*

You extol water in *everything* you see?

Especially what I imbibe. I attribute all qualities to water's fine example. What began from the drop? A lonely little water drop? In a drop, there's a Fall. Man's Fall. And all things surrender to the sea. *(They silently take one more sip as the curtain comes down, after a short, but fluid, interval.)*

A SEASONAL DISPUTE, WON BY THE OVERDRESSED SURVIVOR ON ACCOUNT OF TIME

(Spotlights dissemble torrid sun shadows of tropical intensity.)

(Wiping perspiring brow; dressed in light summer clothes:) God, what a sunny day! *(To audience:)* Sorry to dwell on the weather, but it's the

hottest current subject I can think of . . . Look, there's Roger. *(Roger appears laden.)* He's dressed too warmly. He's wearing a bulging coat. It practically drags him to the ground. It weighs him like a hoary oak.

Hey, what are you looking at me like that for? I'm no freak!

You're dressed so warm . . .

I'm dressed all right. Don't criticize me for the way I dress. It's the *weather* that's all wrong, it's too warm for what I'm wearing.

But you must adjust. The *weather* won't change; *you*'ll have to.

Don't give me your wise benefits. When I want advice, I'll *ask* for it.

But you're uncomfortable! I hate to see you suffer, with such obvious tenacity!

I'm not suffering. I'm waiting.

Waiting? What for?

For winter. To vindicate this coat.

You have a long wait. Aren't you *burdened* with the coat, meanwhile?

It's only a *seasonable* burden.

Not *seasonable*, nor *reasonable*, neither.

Well, the coat stays on. Winter will not catch me unprepared.

But you're too early, if you're a day.

(Dogmatically:) It's *never* too early!

(Urgently:) I must inform you: It's only summer!

Only! Tell my *coat* it's "only." My coat is sweltering!

(Frantically imploring:) Take it off, in mercy to skin and cloth!

But then winter will blow itself into the present, like a shot!

(Desperately reassuring:) It can't. *Autumn's* barrier will intervene, a delaying tactic, till you can put your coat back on.

You never give up; and *still* you haven't convinced me!

Catch my advice while it's hot!

(Resignedly:) Given time, it will cool off.

(Sadly:) Oh. You *are* chilling.

Yes. Be more tepid, and walk off.

(They walk off the stage, garbed as before. A curtain painted of wintry icicles comes dashing down with brisk shivering and snowflakes shuddering off, once given a decent autumnal interval to prevent exposed extremes from neutralizing each other.)

(Brief pause. The characters return to the stage, in front of the meanwhile unlifted curtain. Roger struts, in his heavy coat.)

(Enthusiastically gloating:) I fit the season, I fit the season!

You told me! Why don't I take warnings? I'm not dressed right! My bones have *already* contracted their chill!

Who's right, *now*?

(Shivering:) You are.

Yes, my time has come. Ah, what a *fitting* time! *(Patting his stuffed coast with a bolstered snugness of security, he prances in glee. Behind him, the other falls down like a frozen log, fatally underdressed. The wintry curtain advances, toward the front of the stage, sweeping over the prone victim, who is now behind the curtain, while Roger exults in front, like a ski maniac on a blizzardly mountain. The one protracted shiver of convulsion, the play closes, with a storm's driven ferocity, inhumanely furious.)*

A DOCTOR ILLUSTRATES HIS THESIS
(*What* Thesis? Consult Text, For Answer.)

Two characters: undoctor and doctor.

Doctor, what cure is there for death?

None, I'm afraid.

Couldn't I go to the spa for the mineral waters? Or take more vitamin pills, exercise, change my diet, inhale the mountain air?

Death would laugh at these futile endeavors.

Well, the Grim One at least has *some* humor.

Notice at whose expense.

Doctor—you hardly cheer me up.

I would, were death to change. But it's inflexible. Rigid. Sour-minded. Unyielding. Obdurate. Unflinching. Committed. Rock-bound. For the ages.

You make death sound like a God.

It is: with power over life . . . When life avails not, in its limited power, *God* is there, to show life's limited power. Death is the remaining power, once the limited power finishes. *Before* the limited power finishes, Death is quite there, as a presence-of-mind. What limits us—He has all the rest. Excuse me, I'm weak.

(Doctor faints. He's dead.)

(Undoctor looks aghast.) What final power death has! I tremble *too*, in my knees. My knees buckle. I drop to them. In praying position.

(Death accepts the prayer, spares for a while the undoctor, who remains down on his knees, in his limited power remaining.)

A GIMMICK FOR A COMEBACK

(A comeback from death by the writer of this, with the readers' active cooperation to help revive the dead writer by a mental bridge across death: the passion of curiosity to find a problem completed that was begun by one and engaged in at that one's invitation by the hosts, swelling ranks, of

succeeding readers who live after this work's author is dead and so haul him back in, by virtue of this paper and the cooperative nature of the problem, to life, mentally considering. He's left his mind here. He hopes to reclaim it. Keep his mind warm, meanwhile. It's in your hands, readers.)

Why is it that some things get said whereas others just don't seem to have a spokesman?

That some things get remembered whereas others don't? What law's in operation here? Is it similar to the law operating in the paragraph above?

Locate these mysteries at their sources. Wipe them out, bring them to light. Take a lifetime, if necessary, to complete this assignment. But have other lines of interest, as well, so as not to despair by making no progress in *these* tough mysteries I've set you to solve. Continued failure debilitates: the ego's demoralized. Undertake things you can succeed in, to fortify you in the confidence to take on, persist in, carry through, the above assigned tasks—no child's-play, and better pursued when you're bolstered and braced by successes on the side—fool! For what you succeed in is *thereby* easy.

What you fail in is *proven* hard. (For you, anyway. For others may succeed at what you fail in; as others fail at what you succeed in.) The relative difficulty or ease is not only in *what's* pursued, but in *who's* doing the pursuing.

Then *who* are you? Tell me who. That will have a telling affect on the result. *Who* does it? Who doesn't attempt? Who attempts but fails? And at what?

At the tasks I've set. Why are some things said and others not? Some things remembered and others not? What laws are entailed, in each different case? And who are you, to take on the assignment? And who am I, to set it? And what is this, a paper? A mysterious personal essay? A bold little burst of philosophy? A psychology thriller? A fiction vignette or suspense sketch? An enigma unscientifically sound? A blow on the head? A scratch on the brain? A ray of an idea? Or something broken off, with the part broken off picked up in your head; and what remains, lodged in mine, there to fade, as you ponder. All readers help me. Complete this when I'm dead. The force may revive me; as curiosity explodes death, washes it away, demolishes it to ruins, to set up my return. We have a passion to *complete* what we've put aside, if the spark may be rekindled later. That will resuscitate me. But breathe life, reader, into this: it may be mine, posthumously.

Allowing me to come back! And haunt you! And find out the result of all your findings in the problems set up. Give me your mental help across death: we may link minds, and carry me back across, joining you in life. That's why I've assigned you this. What would it be, without *me*?

THE JERKY-WORKING INVENTION

He was very sensitive about his personal body odor. From armpits, groin, feet, and anus. A local stench from everywhere. On him.

Others were also sensitive about his personal body odor. It was *particularly* offensive to their *noses*. It ruined his popularity appeal, and neutralized his magnetism.—It gave rise to complaints.

But recent history notes that he *did* something abaut it.

How timely, practical, and convenient! What was it?

He invented a highly potent antidote.

By what method did it work?

It was a deodorant spray. By chemical magic.

Did it make the ugly smell go away?

No, it failed to do that.

Then of what uae was it? It didn't do its most essential purpose!

No, but it wiped *him* out. It eliminated all of his physical being, it made him completely invisible, it rubbed him out, it eradicated him, there was nothing left of him, except for one trace: only one remnant, he left. Guess what it was.

His *stink*? Only his stink remained?

Yes, Somehow, he couldn't get rid of it. So it got rid of him, By using him to invent that treacherous weapon that turned against him in an act of betrayal, to preserve only his mortal enemy—more than preserve it: *immortalize* it. He left behind a permanent odor. His own. As his sole testament of his former life. All his survivors recognize him by it, at once, It immediately identifies its former owner. Through it, he endures.

VAMPIRES, OR THOUGHTS OF THEM

What makes me think of vampires?
Vampires.
What else makes me think of vampires?
Thinking.
Because they were there.
By "there," *where*?
In your thinking about them.
You mean only on my mind?
It's not "only": your mind is *everywhere*.

CONVERSATIONS FROM THE INBOX

SOMEONE ASKS WHAT—REALLY—LIFE IS.
THE OTHER DOWNPLAYS HIS ANSWER, IN THEIR BRIEF DIALOGUE.

In a nutshell, what's life?

You're already demonstrating it, just by being.

Being what? Am I life's essence, illustrating it as far as its quintessence?

If you're living, you're a minimum candidate as an exponent to life.

But mentally, can I get my hooks on it?

You cerebrally on the outside wish to fathom the intimate inside living of life, pulse and all, with the whole nervous system lit up like an electric pinball machine, and the brain's insides on full display in their miraculous variety? You're trying too hard. Good luck to that.

You dismiss my project, out of hand?

I don't mean to be discouraging.

(*Sarcastically:*) Oh, no? not? Some things remembered and others not?

IN THIS DIALOGUE, A WOMAN HAS MADE HER CHOICE.
THE REJECTED BEAU OBJECTS, WITH INCREASING VEHEMENCE.
HAMMERING HER POINT HOME, TILL THE REJECTED BEAU IS
DRILLED BETWEEN THE EYES, THE WOMAN IN QUESTION AFFIRMS
HER EMPHATIC CHOICE OF "BUTCH" AS HER HUSBAND-IN-WAITING.

(WOMAN) I'm really sorry. I've got to think of myself. It's no use, in your case.

(MAN) But I love you!

I just can't reciprocate. Butch and I are by the minute getting more and more involved. It's really at the serious point.

No, can't you forget about him?

No, we're deeply involved. It's at a crucial point.

Me! Can't you concentrate on *me!* What about *us.* Didn't we establish *us?*

I know you're desperate, but I only care about him.

You led me on! We got involved. I'm at the pitch of irrelevance?

I'm sorry. It's Butch, not you.

You seemed so sincere about me! You *swore* I was your one!

Don't whine. Sorry, I got involved with both of you. I hedged by two-timing, making sure that at least I'd secure one of you. Then Butch got ahead and stayed there. He's my husband-in-waiting.

Where does that leave me? I mean *us*?

"*Us*" means only Butch and me.

It used to mean me!

He caught up with you and ran ahead. It's only him.

I'm in despair.

You're a rejected lover. I'm better off, so forgive me.

I return cruelty with cruelty, and curse you both till the end of the earth.

That's not due for years yet.

Then so is my revenge, with its slow but wrathful oath.

From which Butch will protect me, in his official post as husband-in-waiting.

IN THIS DIALOGUE: A MAN'S WIFE IS FINALLY DEAD, FREEING HIM TO RESUME HIS OLD AFFAIR WITH HIS SOMETIME GIRLFRIEND ON THE SIDE. BUT LOOK WHAT'S NOW TRANSPIRED. YOU CAN NEVER TELL.

Now that your wife is dead, can't you and I start all over again, since the coast is clear?

Well, yes. It seems ironic. My wife used to say, "Over my dead body," when I confessed my wish to leave her for you. And now she finally *does* have an available dead body over which I can jump back to you, with the coast clear and open, when that old last-ditch possibility has finally returned to feasibility of the "dead body" issue.

Stop enjoying the irony of this long-disputed situation, and take the real step—now that your wife's funeral is over—to resume freely with me.

But I'm still in mourning for her.

But it's been months, and all this time we're both aging a bit at a time.

I can't start returning to you till my mourning for my wife completes itself.

I'm too impatient to wait longer. Meanwhile, Alvin is in the picture.

Who's Alvin?

My new beau.

Then it's over between us. You didn't wait long enough.

Oh, I thought our love had precluded and transcended that old bugaboo about "time."

(Philosophically:) The reassertion of time as a real incidental or accidental interferer in the affairs of humankind, not only now but then: It brings eternity to mind, and other such considerations.

DIALOGUE IN THE "WHAT IF?" CATEGORY, CONCERNING DARWIN AND THE OTHER EVOLUTION ENGINEERS, EXAMINING THE PLEASURE / PAIN PRINCIPLE.

What would have happened if Darwin and the other evolution engineers, after tinkering and tampering, had inserted pain in place of pleasure in all the cases of humans performing sexual copulation?

That would have not only devastated but annihilated the human population, costing you and me and everyone else our very lives themselves.

Then we're lucky that this adverse scenario has never happened. We'd all be dead.

It wouldn't have even gone that far, to the point of being dead. It would have been pre-empted in the first place by never even having been born.

What a loss!

Loss!? That's putting it mildly.

Yes. We shouldn't under-stress the point.

What would have happened to evolution?

A non-starter. Evolution is not only about, but depends on, people.

Like us?

Our species, our race.

In person?

Who else?

A SITUATION TERRIBLE FOR THE ABANDONED WOMAN; APOLOGETICALLY AWKWARD FOR HER ABANDONER. TOLD BY DIALOGUE.

But I love my wife! I can't leave her!

But then how did we get so intimate?

It was circumstance. I was here, you were available, I was attracted, you reciprocated, then things got out of hand. I was crazy about you, but now it's time to return to reality and to my wife.

But *we're* reality! We're the new reality!

My heart yearns back to return to my wife and resume our secure love. You, it turns out, were my circumstance stop-gap intermediate love on my enforced business vacation. But that's over, and the memory of my wife beckons me.

But I took up your whole life here. You can't just drop me, abandon me, leave me.

I must. Necessity turns to reality.

But hadn't we established—

Only briefly. I'm tugged home.

That's cruel! What about me?

It's time for the bus to the plane.

I'll be sitting next to you, sobbing, till you get on line for the plane.

In parting, I can't promise you hope. That would be hypocrisy.

Only hypocrisy could console me.

IN THIS DIALOGUE, SOMEONE IS STUCK IN SADNESS. HIS FRIEND COMPASSIONATELY SHOWS CONCERN AND TRIES TO HELP. THEY FINALLY ROOT DOWN WHAT MAY BE THE PROBLEM.

Preserve yourself from a severe case of melancholy. How long has your depression lasted?

Since I don't know when. When it first hit me, I was already down in the dumps.

Any ostensible reason?

No. Life just wears me out.

That doesn't enlighten me with a specific explanation. What were your particular sets of circumstances?

I can't really account for them. Can't a depression come from a pure lack of a cause?

Are you in the "crazy" category?

Now we're entering mysterious realms of pathology, of inexplicable causes.

You're without a girlfriend. You're too lonely.

Now you're stabbing at the obvious, trying to track down an explanation.

Well, I've got to start *some*where. I don't want to throw my hands up in despair.

You're trying to help me, to talk me out of this, or to track down what's wrong. I'm the patient at hand. It's *my* problem.

Well, as your friend, I got involved.

Are you playing the role of a psychoanalyst?

I seem to be. It's become *our* problem. In the early stage.

Your empathy isn't lightening my load.

Are you accusing me? Or appreciating me?

Neither. I'm lost.

Let's not let your melancholy, now seemingly insoluble, dent our friendship with accusations just because I've jumped onto your case with real concern. Should I leave you alone?

No. Stick by me.

I'm with you. All the way.

Let's address the woman problem?

Well, why not? What's wrong?

I assume a melancholy air, but women don't rally around that. They prefer me lively.

Then change your character. Adjust to their taste.

But character is the feat of a long time, while adjustment is a jump in time.

Attune your rhythm to women. Shop at their market.

But they're not all alike.

Separate one. Then stick fast to her. Squeeze all the intimacy you can get out of her, till in desperation she loves and marries you.

That's too close. I'm allergic to intimacy.

I'm daunted by that handicap, in resolve to help you.

Your help so overwhelms me, I'm moved enough to undergo a radical change and pour the credit on you.

I accept such endowment. Go ahead and earn your gratitude.

A WOMAN DISSUADES AN ARDENT WOO-ER FROM FRUITLESSLY PURSUING HIS SUIT.

(MAN) Adoring you is an exercise in masochism. The more ardent my love, the weaker is your response, which has no pulse or heartbeat in it.

(WOMAN) The handwriting is on the wall, evident to all, that my extreme indifference to you as a candidate lover ridiculously overbalances your foolishly ill-advised ardor. Give up.

(MAN) I have no chance, whatsoever, in reversing the totality of your negativity?

(W) Giving up is my wildly recommended advice. I have no capacity to express it more vehemently, having failed Literary Rhetoric in my college course of Creative Writing.

(M) Who was your instructor?

(W) Marvin. He failed to make me into much of a writer.

(M) Well, he must have tried.

(W) Yes, as *you* now try to win my love, with effort that I laugh and laugh at, bringing ridiculousness to a new record pitch.

(M) Must you ridicule me?

(W) It's persuasively necessary. Marvin taught me that much.

UNDRAMATICALLY UNEVEN DIALOGUE. ARDENTLY IN LOVE, BUT SORELY UNREQUITED, A LOVE-OBSESSED WOO-ER RELINQUISHES HIS PURSUIT: INTELLIGENTLY REALIZING ITS DOOM-FILLED USELESSNESS IN PITILESS FUTILITY'S FITFULLY FRUITLESS RUEFUL EPITOME.

(MAN) Your indifference appalls me. Since my love for you is at extreme intensity, why can't you at least love me back, even if your reciprocation is weak and lacking in energy?

(WOMAN) I don't care for you, so our so-called love is ridiculously unbalanced: everything from you, nothing from me.

(MAN) Do you advise me to give up in futility?

(WOMAN) Not only do I advise it, but urgently recommend it.

(MAN) If I persist, it's a travesty? I'll be hurt, and you won't care?

(WOMAN) I'm not heartless. But so far as romance goes, my heart has no beat for you.

(MAN) Well, I'm beaten. *(Shrugs and gives up, in shrunken posture, arms flailingly outstretched.)*

A FRIEND OF A VICTIM OF MOLLY'S ROMANTIC REJECTION LOYALLY REDUCES MOLLY'S STANDING IN THEIR COMMUNITY BY CITING HER HEARTLESSNESS, HELPING THE VICTIM TO WIN A MEASURE OF ASSISTED WRATHFUL REVENGE.

(FRIEND) Love can be uneven.

(VICTIM) So much so, that one side may command a total monopoly of it, and the other be totally lacking in it, with a response too puny to call itself even remotely a requital.

(FRIEND) That lack of balance surely dooms the pursuit by the ardent lover to abject failure.

(VICTIM) That was my experience. My adoration of Molly is a prime

example.

(FRIEND) Did you arouse nothing but cold-bloodedness in Molly's heartless indifference?

(VICTIM) She also mocked me, and lowered my stock in the community with lowered reputation by rumoring it into the crowd of our age group.

(FRIEND) That social reinforcement of private rejection verged on cruelty. My opinion of Molly as a decent human being has plunged below even the sidewalk's narrow depth.

(VICTIM) Thanks for championing me in my abject failure as the aspiring would-be lover of heartless Molly.

(FRIEND) As a recipient of your sorrowful confession, I'll loyally lower Molly's reputation abysmally among our social peers.

(VICTIM) As a friend, you show me the heart that she lacks.

(FRIEND) But she *does* have a heart—for Bob, her new lover.

(VICTIM) In my envy of Bob, let's ruin *his* reputation too. Thus spreads my wrath.

A DATE MOMENTARILY CANCELED DUE TO VERBAL INCOMPATIBILITY, ONLY TO BE RESCHEDULED DUE TO PATRIOTIC HARMONY.

(MAN) You look juicily sexy. Can we do *(Slyly insinuatingly:)* "you-know-what"?

(WOMAN) Not now, since I'm in the raging midst of my "period," known as "curse" during times of missed opportunity, such as now. Could I have a rain-check?

(MAN) (Hiding his disappointment:) Certainly. When?

(WOMAN) Tuesday.

(MAN) Okay. It's a date—but what if it doesn't rain?

(WOMAN) Don't be literal-minded. I was only being metaphorical. It was a figure of speech, that word "rain." It's been around for ages.

(MAN) Of *course* rain has been around for ages, ever since there was ever any climate or weather announcement on this planet Earth.

(WOMAN) Let's cancel Tuesday's scheduled date.

(MAN) (Disappointed:) But why?

(WOMAN) You have a stupid brain, in your literal-minded absence of metaphorical savvy.

(MAN) But I was born in another country.

(WOMAN) Being an immigrant is no excuse. You can't hide behind the fact that you're a foreigner.

(MAN) I only *used to be* a foreigner. Now I'm American.

(WOMAN) Prove your patriotism.

(MAN) (Starts singing the national anthem.)

(WOMAN) Okay, you win. Tuesday is back on again.

(MAN) Good. Patriotism pays off.

DIALOGGING: SOMEONE TRYING TO HELP SOMEONE ELSE OUT, BUT SO FAR NOTHING SEEMS TO WORK.

How's life treating you?

Badly. I confuse what I should complain about *when*.

Your problems get muddy in overlapping?

I'm no sooner done with one mess, I'm in another.

Can't you give order to your messes?

No, *they* order *me*, and mess around with *me*.

Do you confuse what solutions to apply appropriately to what problems?

My problems get wrong answers, to overload their already excessive complications with further intertwining twisting in convolutions.

Looks like you have to straighten things out.

Yeah, but how?

Oh, you're too solution-oriented. That's what makes you so problematic.

Does your diagnosis yield any advice?

Yes, take on a new outlook. Try a different approach.

Should I blame you if I fail?

I'm nobody's scapegoat.

AN ARGUMENTATIVE DIALOGUE, LEADING TO DISHARMONY AND NO DEFINITIVE RESULT AS TO LIFE'S REAL TRUE MEANING.

What actually is life?

Being alive. But no more questions.

I want to get to the heart of the matter.

This is only conjecture and speculation. Don't bother me about definition.

You're giving up?

Sure I am. Don't bother me.

You're not being co-operative.

I said to shut up.

Are you anti-intellectual?

No. I just can't handle your questions.

Then don't be my friend.

I'll gladly part with you. For the life of me!

Life! What is that you're talking about and what does this "life" word mean?

You're tricking me so I can define life down to its true quintessence? No.

Well, let's be friends. I accept your limitations. But you don't try enough to give me the upshot as to what life really means.

It's clad in mystery. I can't lift its obscure iron curtain or later winding sheet.

My curiosity is superior to yours.

Then its force should provide its own answer.

I tried parasiting on you first.

Well, that didn't work. Then do it yourself, now.

Here goes. *(Looking high up.)* I summon Life's essence, in person.

(Obediently, Life appears, in humble human guise, looking like an ordinary guy.) Hello, I'm Life. You summoned me. Why?

I'm trying to fathom what you really are.

(LIFE) A Greek said, "Know thyself," but I'm damned if I do. Figure it out for yourself.

But I'm a mere mortal.

(LIFE) So am I. Does that help you?

A DIALOGUE THAT STARTS WITH HOPE AND ENDS SOLVING NOTHING, POSSIBLY SPOILING FRIENDSHIP, UNLESS THE CONCLUSION ENDED DIFFERENTLY.

(GEORGE) I know how to maintain a steady level of happiness.

(PETER) Don't keep it secret. If you're my friend, share it with me.

(GEORGE) Lower your expectations. Don't want so much.

(P) But those are generalizations. There are so many different categories, circumstances, situations, even contingencies. No one rule pertains to them all.

(G) Oh, stop complicating things. You're messing up my theories, that are so neat and artistically simple that you shouldn't interfere with my easy formula of solving anything.

(P) Reality doesn't agree with you, being so full of particularities, each of which has to be considered one at a time when it comes up.

(G) You've just ruined my happiness. I thought I had everything figured out, all at once, in one simple grand theory. I was going to generously share it with you, and you were going to be grateful and be in my debt. You spoiled it all.

(P) I apologize, you simpleton. Have I spoiled our friendship?

(G) Only temporarily. Life isn't over yet.

(P) Good. Let's try a different tack.

(G) What different tack?

(P) It depends.

HE LOVES HER. SHE SAYS NO. HER WORD IS FINAL, AND REMAINS SUCH, DESPITE A NEAR FATAL HITCH.

(MAN) I propose love to you.

(WOMAN) I reject it. You're not my type. Besides, I'm engaged to my fiance, whom I love and he loves me. So you're out of the picture, altogether.

(M) I hate being rejected in my love-suit. Can you possibly spare me a little hope?

(W) Categorically, no. I reject you completely. Don't linger. Leave.

(M) If I kill myself, you'll have blood on your hands.

(W) Don't be melodramatic. It won't work.

(M) Is your heart absolutely steeled?

(W) My mind is made totally up. You have no recourse. Your self-assassination would solve nothing, unless to complicate matters further, by being a nuisance for me, as a futile form of revenge that achieves nothing except your own demise as a victim of these pathetic circumstances.

(M) Your eloquence has won me over, and saved my life. Will that alter your rejection of me?

(W) Cold-heartedly, no. I'll still marry my fiance, and you'll still now go on living.

(M) Since I've self-retained life, is there any chance of reversing my hopelessness in the case of your having already turned me down?

(W) None whatever. My rejection remains final.

(M) Well, at least I've got my life.

(W) Yes, but without me. Will you swallow that?

(M) It's a hard pill to take. It contradicts that "Where there's life there's hope."

(W) Get yourself another woman.

(M) Women are not interchangeable. There's only one you.

(W) Thanks for singling me out. But we must part on the terms we started with, but with the big bonus that you retain your life. Does that console you?

(M) Not when I imagine what my life would be with you close in it.

(W) *(Sarcastically, mean-spiritedly:)* Wouldn't you like to know, even hypothetically? *(They part forever, with herself in a false "bitch" role which time will smooth or soothe over, with the humane consolation that his life goes on by theoretical assumption.)*

A MAN IS INTIMIDATED TO WRETCHEDNESS BY BEING PUT DOWN BY A DOMINATING FEMALE, WHO PRACTICALLY DESTROYS HIS FORMERLY SELF-RESPECTING EGO.

(WOMAN) Can we have a brief affair on an interim basis, because my real boyfriend is away out of town temporarily?

(MAN) It flatters me that you consider me for that "plug the gap" role, but also *un*flatters me that you don't visualize me in a substantial front-line role as an actual husband prospect.

(W) I respect you as someone to be taken seriously. You're no slouch.

(M) Then consider me on a full-time basis as full-fledged marriage timber, the towering tree of the forest.

(W) Are you comparing yourself to my true boyfriend who's temporarily away and whose role I foresee as my husband-to-be?

(M) I didn't know what formidable status he had. I'm intimidated and have to give way, humbled in my ranking.

(W) All right, as a temporary you can now have sex with me, I'm ready.

(M) But I'm so deflated, I'm impotent.

(W) Your problem is that you're on an "all-or-nothing" kick. Are you a man or a mouse?

(M) I don't know—we both eat cheese.

(W) Well, *your* cheese has too many holes in it.

(M) You're so much the "I'm-in-charge" type, that my impotence status has gone downhill another notch, thanks to your relentless contempt.

(W) You call yourself a man?

(M) If you recall that I'm relegated to a mouse, let me remind you that mice breed frequently.

(W) Not with *you* at the motor.

(M) As a female, you're too aggressive. If you were a lady mouse, the whole breed would be threatened with extinction.

(W) Your impotence would do that trick adequately.

(M) I'm dutifully chastised. I'll have to creep away with my tail between my legs, entangling me if I try only to crawl away.

(W) You pathetic little would-be excuse for a candidate monster!

(M) Your strident scorn reduces me even further, to insect status.

(W) Your over-all status is in free-fall. At this rate, your reduction will hit the skids.

(M) I've learned my lesson. No more woman like you. Next time I'll woo a very timid, painfully shy virgin.

(W) With *you* on top of her, her virgin status is guaranteed to last her lifetime and beyond.

SHE'S BACKTRACKED.

(WOMAN) It just didn't work out. Forget about it.

(MAN) I can't. I'm obsessed.

(W) Drop the matter. It's done, as far as I'm concerned.

(M) (Pleading:) But we got off to such a good start! What happened?

(W) I made a mistake. I was intrigued by you, but soon I realized you just weren't the guy for me.

(M) But it was so romantic!

(W) I fooled myself. It's my fault. Look, I'm busy. I don't mean to be blunt, but just make yourself scarce.

(M) This is so abrupt. I had an inkling, but this is horrible. Last night, we— *(Woman leaves, leaving him flabbergasted.)*

HE HAS TO SLOW DOWN. SHE TEACHES HIM HOW.

(MAN) I really do love you. Let's immediately marry and have kids.

(WOMAN) Don't be too previous. I'm not that much in a hurry. Calm down. I'm not so certain of you as you are of me.

(MAN) Please catch up with me so we can be on equal footing.

(WOMAN) Give me time. Let's be together a while.

(MAN) Look! Do you love me or not? I can't wait forever.

(WOMAN) Obviously, we have a time problem.

(MAN) Yeah, you lag behind.

(W) It's unfair that your abrupt pace should rule my own tentative and hesitating one. If I'm cautious, be patient.

(M) No. I refuse. I can't wait.

(W) Then you lose me.

(M) That's unacceptable. I'm forced to wait. I'm tamed.

(W) I'm glad you've fallen in line.

(M) You've exercised discipline over me.

(W) (Triumphantly:) Good. You've deserved it.

(M) By being too impetuous?

(W) By eager impulse on a coercive time scale.

(M) Precipitously?

(W) Words, words. Now, relax.

WILL SHE FORGIVE HIM? MAYBE. READ ON.

(MAN) How can we be breaking up when we both love each other? If that's not mutually self-destructive, then what is?

(WOMAN) You've destroyed our love bit by bit with your irresistible

brief affairs. I was waiting for you to stop, but you kept on, like compulsive addiction.

(MAN) Your summary is accurate. I couldn't help it if new women found me irresistible—and I them.

(WOMAN) Yes? With strenuous will power you could have helped it —but you were too weak.

(M) On the contrary, I was too strong. The new women kept coming on, and I proved strong with stamina and endurance to meet them head-on, full bodily.

(W) Congratulations. You took multiple risks, which finally added up to our loss of each other in the item of precious love.

(M) As we share and stare eye-to-eye now, can you bear to break up? I can't.

(W) As I look eye-to-eye with you, I can't bear it. I forgive.

(M) And I stand forgiven.

(W) Let's "do" it.

(M) Sure. I'm recently well-practiced, with lots of rehearsals with relentlessly available understudies.

(W) This is not the exactly right psychological time to boast. I may withdraw my forgiveness.

(M) Yes, but not immediately.

(W) How long will "Immediately" last?

(M) Should I analyze time?

(W) We're too busy now.

(M) Sure. Later. Work comes first.

(W) More like play.

(M) Have it your own way.

SELF-ACCUSATION OF A PHANTOM NON-CRIME? IT'S IN HIS OWN HEAD? GO FIGURE.

(Cast: Nervous Man. His Friend. Passing Cop. Admitting Officer.)

(NERVOUS MAN) My anxiety strikes a high note when a near-by policeman passes by and he's not even looking at me.

(FRIEND) You feel guilty? Of what?

(NERVOUS MAN) Of nothing. His mere presence starts a panic in me.

(FRIEND) But if you have nothing to worry about, why is the panic there? Are you covering something up? Think hard.

(NERVOUS MAN) Stop interfering with my psychic process.

(FRIEND) But I'm your friend. You confessed, rather confided in me, made me curious. I'm just here to help.

(NERVOUS MAN) Ironically, it's causing me further worry.

(FRIEND) Should we drop the matter? Feel better, you're alarming me.

(NERVOUS MAN) There's another cop, and he's coming closer. *(To Cop:)* Officer, I didn't do anything.

(COP) Who's accusing you? What's the matter?

(NERVOUS MAN) You. Why are you walking toward me?

(COP) Just to pass by. That was my direction. I'm arresting you.

(NERVOUS MAN) What for?

(COP) You're in a nervous state. Come along. *(Pointing:)* There's police headquarters. Just a little questioning. I can see you're agitated.

(NERVOUS MAN) Yes, but only because you're here. I got frightened.

(COP) We'll find out why, won't we? *(Leaving friend behind, they enter headquarters.)*

(NERVOUS MAN) I protest! *(Struggling.)*

(ADMITTING OFFICER) What's the trouble here?

NOT SPEAKING UP WHEN THE OPPORTUNITY HAD GLARINGLY BEEN THERE, NOW INFINITELY TOO LATE.

(MAN) Shyness was the culprit. I noticed you decades ago, developed a crush, but circumstances intervened. During the months as they went by, I had periodical urges to conquer my aversion to being too forward, but habitually didn't give in, the result being that I repressed my blurting out my hidden passion.

(WOMAN) I noticed you being conspicuously inhibited. You were hiding an urge, and I felt the moral and selfish need to rescue you and straighten your tongue. But I too held back. We were both in the grips of a fatal reticence. Slowly the months went by, resulting in getting older.

(MAN) Now we each have families of our own—mates and children. We seem content.

(WOMAN) Are we tragic figures?

(MAN) In our combined voices, we may call us that. But let's toughly avoid sentimentality that combines self-pity with mutual loss.

(WOMAN) We can dignify or justify our reluctance to come forward and speak out when the opportunity was wide open and poignantly tempting—even heartbreakingly tempting.

(MAN) Under what guise can we justify or dignify our regrettable silence?

(WOMAN) Modesty. Taste.

(MAN) Politeness. Over-scrupulous consideration

(WOMAN) Delicate refinement.

(MAN) Sometimes coarse bluntness, or subtle directness, wielded early enough, can forge the life-changing combine of romance and marriage.

(WOMAN) May our wrinkles remind us of all that in memoriam. But don't we each love our mates and resultant children therefrom?

(MAN) Yes.

(WOMAN) Then we haven't needed each other.

(MAN) Should that consolation quiet down the "It could have been" regret between the rare combination of you and me?

(WOMAN) It had better. Too late to unravel our current marriages and parenthoods to go on a time planet hypothetical reconnaissance tour.

MUTUAL RECRIMINATIONS REVISITED.
A DIVORCED COUPLE PERPETUATES THEIR DISPUTE
OF DIVERSELY ASSIGNED GUILTS.

(WOMAN) If you hadn't had that marriage-breaking affair some years ago, we'd still be together and even had another child, in place of the barren oasis of our divorce. So your affair was the killer of our possible final child, as well as previously the killer of our very marriage itself.

(MAN) You're assigning too much blame on me. Your extreme reaction and vicious retaliation for my otherwise harmless affair were harshly and vindictively and mercilessly worse than my original offense. You fought back too hard.

(WOMAN) Did you expect me to silently submit with docility to your betrayal of our successfully sacred bond of marriage?

(MAN) I would have expected of course a protest, but not such vehement malice. If you had let my affair take its natural course, it would duly have achieved its normal end, and we would have had each other to resume with again with reinvigorated ardor and mutual respect based on your humble and magnanimous forgiveness and my sincere but abject apologies for my momentary but humanly understandable lapse of absolute fidelity.

(WOMAN) Apparently we're at an impasse as to assigning weights of moral blame to each other. Right is on my side. Wrong is on your side. The battle lines are defined.

(MAN) This sounds like you're still fighting the war ended years ago.

After all, we've both remarried. Don't forget that fact.

(WOMAN) Your betrayal stinks to high heaven with a thousand foul odors that still permeate my outraged nostrils.

(MAN) Your hyper-exaggerations are an insult to rhetoric itself. Your abuse of the English language—

(WOMAN) —Compares nothing with your breaking a devoted wife's heart and ending a fruitful marriage. You miserable—

(Play abruptly ends due to the sudden necessity of sparing the shocked audience from further insults to assaulted play-going sensibilities by abusive language magnifications.)

MONOLOGUE: A LITERALLY ONE-SIDED CONVERSATION.

Well, Jimmy, usually you monopolize the conversation, but this time I have the upper hand—but I'm sorry this has to be.

Now it's your turn to humorously reply, but it's my misery that you're unable to. So I have to fill in—a fool's errand; because you're too dead to respond, much less to hear.

Your appalling silence leaves only me to fill both our parts with wit. But not having you around deprives me of any merriness, where wit may come from.

I must be crazy—I'm talking to a dead person.

But I have to fill in your gaps. Better one-sided than nothingness. At least I imagine the semblance of your old spirit, essence, character, personality, and voice, standing in front of me just the way you used to be. I evoke all these remnants of you. Am I getting nostalgia out of it at least?

No, it's producing melancholy. If our positions were reversed, I'm sure that's how it would be for you, if you were on top of the earth and me under. Am I right?

Your humorous reply has to be left a blank. It's not polite to presume.

HERE'S WHAT HAPPENED—OR RATHER DIDN'T.

If your best friend died, do you replace him by the next in rank?

No, *you* go next, and join him where he isn't, and you're not there either.

So both of you are lost in nowhere, where there's no recognizing each other, in spite of what religion might say or not, in how many words.

So who possesses that great friendship that once *was*, which lasted seventy-five years?

No one, neither you nor your dear old buddy.

It's a lost property, which no one owns, not even by stray kept letters or photos that augmented the real friendship which technically belongs only to the "past," which neither of you two pals can legally or metaphysically claim.

But plenty of other people are currently friends. Their day is already rolling on.

Why are they so blessed? Because they had the decency to get born later, and they're here to enjoy each other—no end?

THE "MELANCHOLY" DIALOGUE.

The flowers that bloom in the spring are welcome to the gladdened heart.

Yet inner melancholy can reduce those flowers and that spring into a state of indifferent irrelevancy.

So melancholy can blot out those natural seasonal charms? That's a big load for melancholy to assume and take on.

Melancholy is capable of burdens of its own making, independent of external circumstances.

Let's dispel melancholy, it's a pain in the ass.

The ass is the least of it. Melancholy can disrupt our whole life systems.

Is there a way of rooting out melancholy?

If so, I'm not privy to it. Melancholy can be pernicious enough to interfere with everything organic that allows life flexibility.

Then my vote is anti-melancholy. It's a visitor that may overstay its leave and corrupt our natural resources.

I can adopt a slogan: "Out with melancholy!"

But can the slogan take effective action?

How far can words go?

Too far. But we need words to negotiate with. Otherwise we're defenseless. Words protect us.

That's why my dictionary is in so safe a place that I can't find it.

Then it must be full of obscure words.

TWO MEN DISCUSS ANTI-WOMEN VIOLENCE.

The only language that women are capable of understanding is the firm, undeniable message of getting beaten.

Aren't you being politically incorrect?

Not the least. Don't be silly. It's well known anthropologically by society at large that women, by constitutionally innate nature, will understand what it means to be thumped hard, even viciously so.

They may well know what it means, but does that necessarily imply that, morally and ethically, men should administer this cruel and unnecessary punishment on women?

You've got a point there.

Well then, will you reform?

How dare you insinuate that I personally beat women!? I'll sue you for every last cent you have, and even make a profit in the bargain.

You're going too far. No need for litigation. You draw conclusions too fast. I went to art school, and they said I could draw anything.

You couldn't even draw the curtains.

Going on insulting me will be curtains for you.

Okay, you've persuaded me. I'm peaceable at heart. I'll stop.

I'm glad to see a man so reasonable. Stop right now?

Sure. Why wait? The most accessibly convenient time for virtually everything is the instant present, the ever-shining "now."

It sure is tempting. I can't wait.

Control, that's what we need. Are you aboard with your co-operation?

So much so, you can't believe it.

Nor can I. Attunement is the most musical blessing.

THE PICK-UP LINE, AND WHERE IT LED TO.
TWO STRANGERS BUMP INTO EACH OTHER ON STREET.

(MAN) Could we have consensual sex together?

(WOMAN) No, I don't know you. But at least you come to the point.

(MAN) But we can get acquainted and then go on from there. Not everything happens at once.

(W) Your pick-up line was too sudden and facile. I'll bet you say that to all the girls.

(M) No, not everyone. I picked you out selectively.

(W) I'm hardly flattered. We bumped into each other on the street accidentally, not preferentially. You didn't even know who I was.

(M) Well, now I do—and you'll do. I had my eyes open. I'll convert random accident into sober and deliberate choice.

(W) How far do you intend to go with me?

(M) Marriage, plus kids.

(W) Would you skip both the introductory stages and the transitional stages in arriving post haste at the point of long-range marital intimacy and painstaking parenthood? Stopping short at the divorce stage?

(M) We could stop to get engaged and commemorate that with a pre-engagement party.

(W) As long as you're making concessions, I want a post-engagement party as well.

(M) You're acting spoiled by asking too much.

(W) This is our first spat.

(M) Well, get over it. There'll be lots more.

(W) You're so volatile. You must forgive me if I feel manipulated.

(M) I'm not that accommodating. We've got to get on with our lives.

(W) Together?

(M) You sound too eager. Now I'll give you the cold treatment. I want you to really love me; and being hard-to-get will inflame your determination to a pitch of desperation—almost despair.

(W) You're too procedural, methodical, calculating—even sneaky.

(M) You're up to speed when it comes to caliber.

(W) Good. Should we start being romantic?

(M) Not so hasty. Putting the cart before the horse is like changing the horse in midstream.

(W) If you confuse me with metaphors, I get bewildered.

(M) Well, by dazzling you I've made a conquest.

(W) Would you betray me?

(M) Only if tempted. By now, you ought to know how impetuously temperamental I am.

(W) *(Wearily:)* I well know. I'm suddenly a veteran.

SOMEONE WAS ORNERY, DIFFICULT, UNCO-OPERATIVE. THE OTHER ONE WASN'T AMUSED.

Life has its sunny side but also its funny side.

I think they're related. Humor tries to make light to alleviate things being wrong, awful, depressing—or fearful.

Yeah; if you're worried or in danger, you may resort to a funny remark or "wise crack" to shed the rotten stuff into a better or different light, prospectively or imaginarily or wishfully.

That's a mouthful. Could you give an example?

No. Find one for yourself.

It's funny that you don't oblige me.

See? That's what I mean.

That means that you're mean.

All I am is just withholding.

Why? Are you ornery? Why be unco-operative?

I wanted to be funny.

Well, that's a funny way to go about it.

That's what I mean. Find humor wherever there's something problematic or difficult or, in my case, hostile. I was trying to excuse myself or play a funny game.

Not so funny from my point. You were just being sarcastic.

At your expense. Somebody has to be on the receiving end.

Maybe you were just being lazy.

Thanks for excusing me.

I was still accusing you. But cut out the funny stuff.

THEY BOUNCE OFF EACH OTHER AND REBOUND TO DO IT AGAIN. AND THAT'S NOT ALL.

A chance remark can set someone off.

Yes, that's how spontaneous we are. One thing can lead to another, quick and erratically.

Our tongues are mercurially lightsilver—or our brains are.

We jump off from one thing to another like quick rebounding flying insects.

Imagination can go zigzag. That's how it can solve problems. Resorting to the seemingly irrational or irrelevant, from odd or unlikely angles.

Surprises: that's what life is full of.

It exploits unpredictability. You can never tell.

But sometimes, contrarily, you *can* tell.

Yeah. That's only common sense.

You figure it out.

TWO MEN, ONE DRESSED ECCENTRICALLY AND THE OTHER NORMALLY.

The wide world of reality is arrogantly hoping to infiltrate my private brain, which I'm trying to protect from unseemly outside influences.

Why not let reality seep in? It may wake you up and do you good.

My unrealistic fantasies are precious to me. I created them through my own efforts; so I must defend them loyally, paternally, like children from my own loins.

But won't your life get into trouble if you keep polluting your brain with your own internal rot that grows stale the more it's repeated and advanced into crooked digressions through your dreadful stream of consciousness?

My eccentricities are protectively insulated from the outside world by infusions of socialistic money from our liberal government. I got on their system exploitingly. So now I'm free to hide behind my fantasies from the intrusions of rude reality.

But doesn't that make you out of step with your fellow human beings socially? Aren't you marching to a different rhythm or drum-beat from anyone else, thus isolating you into being a social hermit, which leads to your being a social misfit, craven with loneliness?

I'll independently go through life in my own private way by sticking to my guns.

Before it's too late, wake up.

Sorry. I'm too far gone.

How did I get granted to conduct this interview?

You didn't. You're only a figment of my imagination.

MAN BUMPS INTO WOMAN BY ACCIDENT, BOTH BEING STRANGERS.

(MAN) Since I love you, can't we marry?

(WOMAN) (Recoiling:) But we only just met!

(M) Then that's all the more romantic, this abrupt suddenness.

(W) But I'm unprepared. I'm startled.

(M) Calm down. This doesn't call for hysteria. Just get used to it.

(W) To what?

(M) To our becoming harmoniously familiar, even intimate, after starting off as abrupt strangers.

(W) But I was already engaged.

(M) Get rid of him. I come first.

(W) You're very insinuating and presupposing.

(M) No, I'm proposing.

(W) You're being impulsive.

(M) All the more dashing. I'm a figure of spontaneity.

(W) *(Standing up to him:)* That doesn't give you any rights over me.

(M) No, but I take them.

(W) You're too impetuous, not to mention arrogant.

(M) Under the circumstances, what else could I be?

(W) You're pressing your luck.

(M) Too late to back out. I've hooked you.

(W) I can't let you get away with this arrogant feat of insolence.

(M) Call it what you want. I'm a man of action.

(Inconclusive conclusion, held in suspense.)

TALE OF TWO SOCIAL BEVERAGES. ONE HAS PROPERTY BUT THE OTHER DECLINES PROPERLY TO BE AN INFERIOR VISITOR TO ANSWER A TYRANNICAL INQUISITOR. THE STORY IS WRITTEN IN PROSE. THEY ALMOST SEEM LIKE FOES, COMPARING THEIR SOCIETAL WOES.

Tea paid a social visit to Coffee.

Coffee welcomed Tea: "Can you stay here a while?"

Tea said, "Sorry, no."

"But I invited you," said Coffee, "on my grounds."

Moral: Coffee has grounds, but Tea leaves.

A DIALOGUE CUT SHORT WITH AN EXCUSE.

(A) Life is so risky, I wonder how people allow themselves to get born.

(B) Well, you have to take your chance *some* time.

(A) Is getting born a now-or-never situation?

(B) Yes. It's like some youthful romances, where the situation comes to the crux of the matter: Do they both agree to commit? Or not? If not that time, that might be the last chance.

(A) Yes, there are ripe times. With a young, marriageable girl, her time may have come, if the right man proposes.

(B) If he doesn't, then heartbreak?

(A) Not necessarily. On the rebound, the secondary choice or the compensatory opportunity might fructify into a better marriage than the original or primary candidate would have made.

(B) You never can tell.

(A) Oh yeah? Sometimes you can.

(B) Why are you so contradictory?

(A) That's often the nature of dialogue. Drama, you know.

THE WORM'S VIEW FROM BELOW, ILLUMINATED BY SEX'S GLOW. WILL SPECIES' EXTENSION FLOW? THEY'RE NOT ENTICING, SO DON'T SQUIRM. THIS IS STRICTLY WORM FOR WORM.

(MALE WORM) I warm up to you and wish to marry you to propagate our lowly species.

(FEMALE WORM) I don't know. I'm a virgin.

(M) Well, it's time to get going. The earth is slowing down, so let's get in step.

(F) You fool! You think you're making a conquest? You're not! You're mistaking all of me for the other end of your own coiling body, which winds so far in loops that there's no virtual end of you, for all of enticing me.

(M) By lengthening me, you cut me down to size.

(F) But I'll marry you anyway. What's your cock's extension?

(M) I'm not a mathematical whiz. Go find out for yourself.

(F) All right. Proceed. *(Pause.)*

(M) I'm eager. Are you?

(F) No. I'm shy.

(M) Oh, you're playing the game of female coyness.

(F) Well, it'll work. Prepare for species reproduction.

(M) Forget that. Pleasure is my aim.

DIALOGUE ON LOST ROMANTIC YOUTH. MOURNING THE PAST AS A NEW ENFORCED PASSION, IN PASSING.

I'm so old, women no longer see me romantically. They see me as an old-age caricature of a generic stereotype.

Then give up on them.

But then I'm less than a man.

Yes, but you still have your past.

That's the trouble. I don't have it any more. I'm a used force.

Well, at least you *once* had it.

What good does it do me *now*?

Why are you so dependent on *now*? Any search for such former nows' renewals would be futile. Be content merely to be a has-been, to cut short your wasteful longing for the impossible.

But I mourn its loss.

Then become a connoisseur of mourning. Regard it as a new passion.
Then I'd betray my age.
Didn't your age first betray *you*?
A betrayal I can never forgive.
It eats your heart out?
My heart is already out. It eats the leftovers.

RECONSIDERING SUING.

You know a lawyer?
Yeah, why?
I wanna sue my parents.
They're long dead and you're an old man. What's their crime?
They were too premature in getting me born; that's why I'm so old.
It's not their fault that they impulsively couldn't hold back from sex soon enough for you not to be so excessively old. But who would you sue anyway? They're both dead. You have no case.
You're right. Why waste my time?

POLICEMAN PARANOIA.

(ME) When I pass a policeman, or when he passes me, I get irrationally scared.
(PAL) What's wrong? Are you guilty?
(ME) No. I'm innocent.
(PAL) So what's the problem?
(ME) It's just the power he possesses. He's authorized to arrest people.
(PAL) But you're innocent; why be scared?

(ME) He's loaded with a gun. He may turn on me suspiciously. He could do something crazy to me.

(PAL) Policemen bring out your paranoia.
But must it annoy ya?
What if he's not for ya?
He could destroy ya.
It makes you neurotic.
He could be despotic
and represent the demotic.

(ME) You're making a crazy rhyme out of my fear?

(PAL) I'm trying to make your fear disappear.

(ME) You're my doctor to cure me.
Please do reassure me.

BETTER TOO MUCH WEATHER THAN NO WEATHER AT ALL, WHETHER OR NOT. LET RAIN REIGN. IT DOESN'T FEIGN. IF YOU'RE INDOORS, THERE'S NO PAIN.

If the rain is dithering what to do or stop or turn on again, what can us people to do? Self-regulate? I guess we'll have to struggle along and not use the rain for any ulterior purpose except letting it go on its own irregular ways and not bother our lives with human-derived maxims that serve no one's use, and leave the rain on the side because it's all wet anyway, so leave it to itself to dry up and just be a side issue as far as we're concerned. Indoors are our refuge along with other purposes, but I'm not an architect.

AN UNEQUAL DIALOGUE: MAN AND WOMAN.

(HE) Simply put, I love you.

(SHE) That's not enough. Your Superior Rival has won me. Relinquish

your desire.

(HE) I so envy him! He values you less than I do. With your consent, I'd gladly marry you. Yet my Superior Rival won you with the limited promise of only sex for a while, leaving you abandoned with no marriage contract whatever.

(SHE) Sex with him tops sex with you, which dooms you in the competition.

(HE) Even when he finally leaves you?

(SHE) In that case, I'll consider you. My role will be the left-over bride.

(HE) Then in revenge and spite, I might mistreat you.

(SHE) No. Leave the mistreating to me. Your Superior Rival will show me how.

THE CAREFUL COWARD.

Being a coward prolongs life, since it helps to keep me out of trouble. It cautions me not to take rash chances that could cause accidents. Being a coward helps me reduce risks, with the reward of further longevity.

What a coward you are!

I'd rather not be called a coward; it sounds demeaning and reduces pride. It's less shameful to be called "careful."

All right, you've salvaged your pride. You're now free to hold your head up high.

You insult me by implying I care how I seem to other people.

Sorry. But that's how you revealed yourself.

I gave myself away?

Yes. That was sheer courage.

UNREQUITAL: THE TWO-GENDER DIALOGUE.

(MAN) I'm too lazy or indifferent to love you, but I wouldn't mind at all if you loved me.

(WOMAN) That sounds like an invitation to be unrequited. Why should I bother?

(M) Can't you summon irresistible passion of love for me, just for its own sake, without requiring the reward of getting requited for it?

(W) Sounds too one-sided. Love needs balancing out of being loved in return for its effort that's so risky.

(M) What about love for its own sake, without the reward expectation that perhaps spoils the purity of initiating love?

(W) No thanks. I'm no saint. No sucker. The solitude of purity makes me shiver with loneliness.

(M) Are you saying that you give up?

(W) Sure. For self-preservation.

(M) You selfish bitch!

(W) That's an unfair accusation.

(M) Who said love is ever fair!?

(W) Can't you trade in your stated indifference in return for whipping up a generous passion for me?

(M) The passion of lust, yes. The passion of love, no thanks.

(W) You selfish male!

(M) Are you insulting my gender!?

(W) No. Only you.

SO ABRUPT, STEP BY STEP.

(HE) Your love for me is uncalled for. What precipitated it?

(SHE) Simply that you seem my type.

(HE) Well, you're not mine. Let's be cordial, but no more.

(SHE) If you give me a chance, we could develop a bond.

(HE) Which I have no desire for. I resent what you insinuate to try to initiate. You seem to jump at me out of nowhere.

(SHE) I don't mean to impose. I propose we go on a date, then go on from there.

(HE) You're projecting something on me I have no appetite for. Have you been hiddenly sighing about me for a while? In fact, I feel spied upon. Your antennae are all over me.

(SHE) In first an imaginary embrace, then a real one.

(HE) Keep your distance. Are you propositioning me?

(SHE) Emphatically. Can't you feel the heat?

(HE) Too close for comfort. Back away.

(SHE) No. Try and prevent me.

(HE) You seem obnoxiously assertive. But it turns aggressive.

(SHE) That's my only recourse, to win you over.

(HE) Well, if you want me that badly, what are you offering?

(SHE) My entire body, then marriage.

(HE) What are your credentials?

(SHE) My past is none of your business. Why are you panting?

(HE) Lust.

(SHE) Well, that's a first step.

NEW YORK SNOWBALL ARGUMENT.

It's spring now.

So I've observed. It's all around. What about it?

The winter just ended.

How brilliant of you. What about it?

It never snowed!

I'm not surprised. New York City isn't always a successful candidate to attract snow, even in the prime of winter.

But that's a crime against nature, for our city to be so bypassed! I'm indignant!

You have no power to compel our city to attract snow, even in winter.

Of course not. Either it snows or it doesn't. I'm no dummy.

New York is powerful, but even *it* has limits in the art of persuasion.

You mean the art of magnetism.

Snow has a will of its own, in where to alight.

I'm a proud New Yorker, and insist on my city getting its fair share of rugged outdoor nature, such as what snow provides.

You're too chauvinistic. Are you suing New York?

No, the weather indicator, or climate interferer.

You're tampering with nature, with that kind of magic thinking.

Nature is a lazy bum to neglect New York as a proud dumping ground for occasional remnants of invigorating, manly snow leftovers.

Are you crazy?

No, snow is. Think of all the invaluable publicity it would get by including the most famous city in the world for snow-snaring! A proud endorsement!

Snow isn't that great a catch: It's bound to melt.

Like you, with an argument that's all wet.

THE OLD MAN AND HIS FORMER PUPIL. THERE'S LIFE YET. POIGNANCY REVISITED.

You were my lifelong crush, beginning at school where you were my gym teacher. Now that we've accidentally re-met, is it too late to somehow marry?

No, I'm too old. I've been through too much already in my rather worn-out life. You'd be my nurse rather than my wife.

Just to cherish you would be my lifelong dream.

Can you keep me alive an extra inch?

Such is my girlhood dream. Life has gotten away for both of us, but it's not too late.

All right, let's do it, at the verge of my life's demise.

Just last-minute rescue of your dear lost life is my only remaining dream.

But I've lost vigor.

Are you referring to impotence?

Yes, the dread of all men, it's finally overtaken me in permissible old age.

Whatever, now that I've found you, you're mine. A realized girlhood crush. Pulling you out from a plunging verge. It'll realize my life.

What a martyr! But I'll take you on.

Do you remember me from school days? I placed an apple on your desk.

No. But welcome at the end. Did I eat it?

I presume so, my darling.

Well, there's more left. What's my new wife's name?

1. OLD MAN.
2. YOUNG MAN ATTEMPTING TO CONSOLE HIM.

I love life, but feel terrible about having old age maladies getting increasingly worse, thus dragging me to an inevitable death I'm too helpless to resist.

That's a terrible—but common—predicament among the vulnerable elderly. So why complain? You're trapped in this common mess; no way out except to die.

Well, I protest.

It's an ineffectual protest, of no avail whatever. You share the common lot. Welcome to the crowd.

I like to be unique, and not conform to the conventions.

Admirable to feel unconventional, but you can't back it up by putting it into action.

So I'm stuck?

Sadly, that's the case.

I can't squirm my way out of it?

Realistically, no.

Then I'll resort to becoming insane, and live in my own world of denial and illusion, not to mention fantasy.

Good luck. If you ever have time enough to return to sanity prior to death, be sure to let me know.

I'll be too crazy to be sure to let you know.

Okay, so forget it. I wash my hands of it.

That makes you so *hand*some.

Thanks for the flirtation, but crazy elderly types like you are not my type.

Too bad. I was getting aroused. Oh, well. Love *often* turns out lousy.

A SPOILED MAN COMPLAINING TO A REASONABLE MAN.

No one understands me.

It's up to you to *make* yourself understood, in no uncertain terms. But be fair-minded.

But they don't pay attention.

Because they can't read your mind. Human relationships are full of give and take. You can't have everything going your own way.

People turn their backs to me.

It's your own fault. Establish relations on an equal basis with others.

Why should I initiate the first move?

They think you're spoiled and self-absorbed. Treat others with respect on their own terms.

Do they deserve it?

Give them a chance to. Make a concession. Be kind and considerate.

If I do, will they treat me fairly?

Some will, some won't. Go out of your way. Give others a break.

Stop bullying me.

If you're in social life, you're not alone. *Relate* to others.

I'm better than others. Why don't they realize it?

You may not be better than some of them.

(Yelling:) Are you on my side or not?!

THE EVER RESTLESS MIND,
VEERING OFF IN ITS GRIND.

If you pursue a line of thought, be prepared to digress. Ideas seem to veer off. You can't just stick to one point you've already made. It inspires restlessness, and seems to lead on along possible diverse paths.

Then it's true what folk wisdom seems constantly to proclaim: that "one thing leads to another."

We connect the dots, so there have to be enough dots to have enough latitude and longitude to make a lot of points.

Like the cloth of a tailor, there has to be enough material to stay in business.

I'll sign on the dotted line.
No wonder we keep a busy mind.
That's the nature of human kind.
Thoughts don't come in isolation.
They admit of constant variation.
They go from one thing to another.
Keep it in the family, or find a new brother.

THE "LEVEL OF CULTURE."

Isn't life more than just a pain in the ass?

Sure. Go into a museum, a library, a musical concert hall, and you can be inspired that life is much higher than a mere pain in the ass.

Thanks for lifting life to a higher level. It gives me hope and inspiration.

Good. I need a lift myself, so I practiced by giving you one.

So as not to be a philistine, let's cultivate culture.

All right. Does that include religion as well?

Religion has to do with spirituality, not culture.

I never considered that distinction. But I'll take your word for it.

Take my word. But I'm not so wise as you give me credit for.

How so? Do tell.

I bought something for a dollar, but miscalculated the amount of change to expect when I paid with a five dollar bill.

Oh, a mathematical error?

No, a financial one.

I never considered that distinction.

Are you as dumb as you look?

Yes, but when I look in the mirror, it's a different story.

How so? Do tell.

Just before looking in the mirror, I shoved a distinguished college professor in front of my path, so that his was the reflection that I saw.

But that's cheating.

Don't be too particular. I need every possible advantage.

I didn't consider your level of desperation. How high is it?

Upon reflection, I consult the mirror, with the professor in front.

But that's only a front.

Don't confront me on this issue.

THE FRIENDLY BUT IRRESPONSIBLE DISPUTE.

To avoid death, I take lots of precautions.

Yeah? Such as what?

Do I have to particularize? No, I needn't bother.

But aren't details necessary for getting your point across?

I assumed that you're sufficiently intelligent to be on my wavelength, so that details don't matter. All you have to do is look at me.

I am. So what?

Don't I look and function alive?

I'm not a doctor; and even a doctor can't just go on assumptions without examining the patient.

Oh, you're the scientific type, always looking for evidence?

You're so suspicious that you demand proof?

Of course. This is the modern age. Every age before us used to be modern, and look what happened: they all died out.

So? What's your point? I'm getting impatient.

Control yourself. If you're so eager, you'll split an artery.

That's a rash assumption. You can get arrested for imitating a false doctor.

As long as you don't turn me in with "citizen's arrest," I'm all right.

You're depending on loyal friendship?

Sure. Aren't you a pal?

Sure. I'll back you up.

Then I'm safe.

Safe from arrest doesn't mean you're right.

What do I have to do? Write an encyclopedia?

Write it!? You can't even spell it.

Don't spoil friendship with insult. Ease off the pressure on me. I'm only human.

That's everyone's excuse.

And a very efficient one, too. You can go far with it.

REJECTING EVOLUTION BECAUSE OF A BUSY LIFE.

Evolution lucked out and came up with a great formula to increase life population on available earth. It invented two separate genders which, magnetized to each other, fornicated and got babies.

To continue: The old were dying out, so the human race replenished its population by replacing the vacancies created by old-age deaths to keep human life going by providing room for new-borns and their parents.

Yes, but how did it all start? My eyes are beginning to glaze over.

Humans evolved from lower life forms like fish and birds that came up from the shore and flew down from the air in phases of slowly evolved body shapes, that gradually came up with, or led to, the human complex organism, still divided into two great genders that loved and lusted for each other with importantly separate genitals that led to romantic intrigues, sometimes competitively.

So this was how we all came about?

Sure. Isn't it a great story?!

Sorry, I'm not that interested. I have my own life to lead, and it's a complicated road to hoe with all my difficulties of getting on, including money and jobs.

Weren't you in awe?

Yeah, but give me a break. This academic stuff is for the birds. I'm too distracted. I have a date with a great dame. I have a marriage prospect!

Good luck. Thanks for your attention.

LIBERATING YOURSELF FROM SELF-CONSCIOUSNESS.

If you're *living* life, how can you analyze it at the same time? Isn't it only one or the other?

No. Analyzing life is as much an integral part of living life as going to work or playing ball, or even kissing someone.

But doesn't life get too self-conscious about itself if it catches you analyzing it?

No. Analyzing is part of life's spontaneous changeability, always on the move.

Okay, life: I'll feel free to analyze you. *(Takes out camera.)* Act normal and natural. Pretend you're posing for the camera, but you don't have to smile if you don't feel like it. *(Snaps camera at himself.)*

How did it come out?

It didn't. The camera is defective.

Well, at least *you're not*. You acted with calm disappointment. Perfectly natural, considering the circumstances.

A FOOT-RACE INTO POLITICS.

At times, life gets too far ahead of me.

Has it challenged you to a foot-race? Then wear more athletic shoes and get slimmer.

No, not *that* kind of race. I mean all the things I have to take care of: my duties and obligations and chores and responsibilities. That's what I mean by life, and I lag behind.

Then go ahead and catch up.

Easier said than done. It's cheap of you to give practical advice, but hard for me to follow it.

You and life are not two things. They're one and the same.

Thanks for that confirmation of identical unity. Divided I fall; together I remain, as a solid entity.

You sound like the United States.

Color me red, white, and blue. Thanks for the patriotic compliment. How do I stand politically?

For liberty and freedom.

With no entangling alliances?

You're married, aren't you?

Entangling alliances mean abroad.

Well, you married a broad.

THE BIRTH DRAMA, FROM BEHIND THE SCENES.
THEY DESPERATELY HAD TO FIND THE MEANS.

(AGENT) The pair of opposite-gendered parents of good stock indispensable for getting born is your available opportunity, starting now, if you act quick.

(*) How do I ignite them?

(AGENT) Create a spark between them.

(*) Have they already amorously readied themselves for my launching?

(AGENT) Go ahead. They've been lusting. But the female is shy.

(*) Get the male to overcome that shyness by persistence.

(AGENT) She's easing into giving permission. Now they're at it. She's giving in.

(*) It's going through?

(AGENT) It's done. You're on the way.

(*) I thought I'd never make it!

(AGENT) As your agent, I despaired.

(*) Nature gave permission?

(AGENT) With the mutually necessary enthusiasm. Getting them to co-ordinate was the trick.

(*) Good old sex. Congratulations.

(AGENT) No. The credit is all yours. I bow out. *(Leaves.)*

DOES A POLICEMAN MAKE YOU NERVOUS?

(Passing each other uneasily: cop and citizen.)

(COP) You looked nervous and guilty when I just passed by. Why?

(CITIZEN) Because of your arresting authority and professional bear-

ing of a gun.

(COP) What have you done?

(CITIZEN) My conscience is clear. My nose is clean. You frighten me by questioning me, but I declare myself innocent. I was just passing by, and froze to see your gleaming badge and ominous uniform, the silent voice of authority. By virtue of my very citizenship, I felt implicated.

(COP) I can see your quivering. I apologize for upsetting you.

(CITIZEN) Your official suspicion made me knuckle under, like a paranoid superstition.

(COP) I release you. Breathe deep and feel confident.

(CITIZEN) Thank you, Officer. I defer to you with anxious deference to accept my gratitude. I'm free, relieved.

(COP) We're both humans. You were pressured by my occupational hazard in spite of being innocent.

(CITIZEN) I take citizen's pride in my innocence.

(COP) You're a model citizen.

(CITIZEN) I'm glad I'm above criticism.

(COP) Don't go crazy and attempt a witticism. It might lead us to a bitter schism.

(CITIZEN) How so, Officer? Haven't we eased off? Why pull rank *now*?

(COP) What's my job for? To take it seriously.

WORLDLY DIALOGUE
SO AS NOT TO BE IN A FOG.

Does "psychology" apply to the individual as "sociology" does to groups?

Yes, but where does "political" come in?

"Political" is ultra-sociological.

Is it divided into parties?

Yes, but no drinking allowed.

There are so many of us people. Our race has proliferated.

No wonder the world is so crowded that it has to be divided first into continents and then into countries.

That's where geography gets itself put on the map.

How does history go?

To hell. The human race has suffered from it.

Yes, but only while it's happening.

The aftermath counts, too.

What can we do about it?

Organize.

Into what? Like picketing with banners and unions? Like rallies and activism?

Don't get controversial. People differ and disagree.

How about co-operation? What's its organizing principle?

Either "My way or the highway," or "We're all in this together."

Universal harmony is idealistic.

Idealism is often unrealistic.

"Human kind cannot bear very much reality," T.S. Eliot said.

I would have too, had I been him.

Don't be so one-uppity.

THE UNFORGIVING WIFE ASSURING ME OF A LOST LIFE. THE PUNISHMENT WAS HARSH. BUT I WAS TOLD TO MARCH.

Being faithful to me being my strictly only wifely demand, which you've violated, I'll launch divorce proceedings.

But I was only under temporary temptation, and never lost my love and respect for you, while simultaneously undertaking my brief breaking of your rule. All I'll ask is wifely forgiveness.

Too late. You married quite plain into money by successfully wooing me. Now that you're losing me, I'll make sure that you're losing financial security as well, in addition to this middle-class, well-upholstered flat.

I was always a helplessly dependent but romantic bum. I had to drag money out of others.

I'm your final "mark." Now you're in the dark.

You have the power to ruin me. Please don't.

I'm inspired with vindictive cruelty. It pleases me to inflict this on you.

But my heart wasn't in it when I strayed. "She" briefly lifted her dress and then I was lost to lust.

Thus making our marriage a bust. Getting down on your knees to repent gives me a merciless burst of satisfaction.

I'll rub it in cruelly.

"She's" too poor for me to get secure consolation by moving in with her and leaching off her as I had been off you.

You were my parasite. Now you're only a pathetic sight. Get off this site.

I repent!

Ill spent! It makes no dent. Delight me by having went. You're a no-good gent. But first I'll assure you'll be broke, financially ruined. I have spoke.

THE CRITIC'S INTEGRITY VERSUS THE NOVELIST'S FAME-CRAVING.

I'm trying to be famous as a novelist. But you as a magazine literary critic condemned my first novel recently as inferior in plot, style, and characters. You're blocking my way to fame. With reviewers like you, I might as well quit writing altogether.

I can't apologize, because I have the integrity to review as I see fit and not be corrupted by doing the author a favor, which you corruptly requested.

I challenge you to a fight, wherein I hit you hard enough for your damaged brain to lose its capacity to write any book review.

Then I sue you for damages.

Then I change my mind and don't hit you, but only curse you. Words can't hurt you.

Yes, but *my* words hurt *you*. That's why you're complaining.

Can't we be friends so that you loyally change your recent damning book review to praising and raving?

No, that issue is already printed, which is why you read it. Are you writing a new novel with better plot, style, and characters, so my integrity will permit a more favorable review next time?

Sure, it's a deal.

Not so fast. I'll only review according to my unbiased opinion.

My integrity intends that.

Then I'll please your integrity by writing so superior a novel, with excellent plot, style, and characters, that your integrity will be obliged to write a review so praising, even adulatory, that my rise to fame will be rousingly launched.

I give no promises.

Well, goodbye, I'm going home to start my next novel. Wish me good luck.

My integrity doesn't permit that.

You cold fish!

That insult passes my integrity test, which now feels fortified.

Good. My future fame will battle your integrity to the finish.

May the best profession win.

FACING FAMILY POWER REALITY – BLOOD THICKER THAN LOVE.

(WOMAN) We'll have to break up.

(MAN) Why? We love each other!

(WOMAN) You're too poor for me. My family is agitating for me to have children to extend our pedigree dynasty to the next generation. You have no money and no career prospects of financial improvement.

(MAN) Why not rebel against your family, and we can marry and live modestly or humbly?

(WOMAN) Because they control me. They have rigorous plans for me.

(MAN) Can't you break away and be independent?

(WOMAN) I'm financially dependent on them. We'll have to separate. The money barrier is impossible to break.

(MAN) My *heart* will break.

(WOMAN) You'll recover and meet another woman.

(MAN) No-one is like you. I love you. I'll get a job and you get a job; and our combined incomes will keep us above the hovel level.

(WOMAN) Sorry. Blood is thicker than love, in our tragic case.

(MAN) Then you don't love me enough?

(WOMAN) I'm a member of my family. We pull together. I'm their way to the next generation. They'll brook no interference. I'm their vehicle. Nothing will stop us.

(MAN) Not even me?

(WOMAN) Sorry. Let's keep in touch.

THE WIFE-BETRAYAL.

I have a personal problem.

As your friend, I'm "all ears."

I love my wife, but I'm being lustfully tempted by a neighboring woman who's making direct hints in my direction.

What a common predicament! Do you meet it directly, or can you squirm out of it?

That's what I need your advice for.

There's no getting around it. Do you love your wife dearly?

Forever. I can't get more emphatic than that!

Then resist the neighbor's temptation.

I'm only human, and a man.

That's no excuse. Temptation or no temptation, you must fight it.

I'm weak. I'm made of flesh.

Don't get sentimental.

What can I possibly do?

As a husband of integrity, resist. As a man of weak flesh, comply with your neighborly temptress.

Are those my only two options?

As far as I can count: I'm not a mathematical whiz. Back to your wife: Is she suspicious?

No.

Then give in to temptation, but make sure she doesn't find out.

I'm too honorable to be a sneak. What do you take me for?

Then will you face divorce?

Her anger would make that probable.

Keep the wife, *and* your honor.

I'll blame your advice when I turn down my neighbor.

If she's that hot, can you fix her up with me?

THE STARKLY HOPELESS DIALOGUE.

So far, so good, but I'm getting worried.

Why?

I'm getting so old. From the example of other people my age, they're mostly all dead by now, some confirmed by obituaries you can actually read. Who am I to be an exception?

You're right to be worried. The body wears down, even though you do physical exercise.

I dread death terribly.

I don't blame you. I being a little younger than you, I'm prepared to be scared too.

From this predicament, what's my solution?

There *is* none, I'm afraid. Just "grin and bear it."

It's not funny. It's heartbreaking. To depart from my still alive wife and good friends is unbearable.

Well, don't kill yourself over it.

Stop kidding me.

Given your current circumstances, I can only weakly resort to humor.

Look at how much laughing I'm doing! It's tragic!

Then resort to magic. Adopt Christ and pray for heaven.

That's unrealistic.

Then you're stuck.

(Awed, dumbfounded silence instead of reply.)

Join the crowd.
But I'm not a conformist.

PATHOLOGICAL DEATH-FRIGHT.

My main problem is that I'm scared of dying.

Are you doing everything you can to live as long as you can? Seeing all your specialist doctors at frequent intervals to check up with different parts of your body? Eating healthy nutrition? Exercising regularly?

Yes, all those things I'm religiously attending to. I'm not negligent in any of those self-duties.

But nevertheless you're still scared of dying?

To a pathological degree.

As long as you're trying to extend your life by all possible vigilant means, you're doing all you can. Nevertheless, you remain scared of dying?

Yes.

Then you're a coward.

Would going to heaven as a religious believer in Christ alleviate my situation?

No, it's too unrealistic. Stick to reality.

Death still frightens me out of my wits.

Then live with it.

With what? Death?

No. Your fright.

I'm too frightened to. I can't fight it.

Of course not, being doomed.

Thanks for your so-called help.

Seek a psychiatrist, not me.

But as my friend, you're cheaper.

Oh, so it comes down to money.

It's the government's fault. There should be free psychiatry for every citizen.

Oh, so it comes down to politics. It's a political issue.

That distracts me from death-fear and fright.

Politics is for nobler purposes.

WHICH TO MARRY? (A FINANCIAL PROBLEM.)

Help me with my problem?

Sure.

Of my two concurrent romances, I half-love a rich marital prospect, and fully love a poor marital prospect. Which should I marry?

How are *you* fixed financially?

I'm poor, without money prospects, being unemployable, and a parasite on others to make ends meet.

Then you have no alternative than to marry the rich marital prospect whom you're only half in love with, and renounce the poor marital prospect whom you fully love.

But fully loving her, my heart would break by having to give her up.

But you can't have it both ways.

Right. That's what problems are for: weighing what you give up for what you gain.

You're so pragmatic!
I can't afford not to be.

MEETING OF TWO HELL INMATES.

Here we are in hell. Hello. What are you here for?
Bad deeds, too horrendous to mention.
Same with me. The religious bosses noticed what I did and punished me accordingly. It's too hot here.
The extra heat is for punishment. Did you deserve it?
It doesn't matter what my opinion was. The religious bosses decided, and that was that.
They obviously had too much power. After serving our terms, will we be released?
Not till eternity is done and over with.
That seems unnecessarily cruel in the length of time.
That's why they call it hell.
Is hell an Anglo Saxon word?
No, English, and it hurts like hell.
The language makes it more severe?
No, it was the power of the religious bosses. They laid it on thick.
And we get it in the neck.
Everywhere else. Punishment is the specialty here.
Ow!

MEETING OF TWO HEAVEN INMATES.

Isn't this heavenly?
That's just the word for it. It's so descriptive!

What are we allowed to do here?

Have free access at any time to our joint harems.

Wouldn't it wear us out?

Heaven gives extra privileges, plus freedom from fatigue.

In comparison with hell, it's a whole different league.

How do you know? Were you ever in hell?

Yes, but boy did I suffer!

That's the nature of the beast.

To say the least.

How did you get out?

Luck. I got switched.

Why?

Good behavior, noticed by the Savior.

Thank God for His observation.

What about *me*? I was the one observed.

An award you thoroughly deserved. But don't you give Him credit too?

He's the famous one, but life is all about me.

PURGATORY.

What are you doing in Purgatory?

Getting purged of my sins, or you could call them crimes. And being decided on as to what's my next step: Heaven or Hell.

That's a major decision. Can you influence the voting?

I could manage maybe to put in a word edgewise.

My previous advertising career could maybe be decisive for my persuading skills.

Good luck. Heaven could be your lucky break.

But hard to live up to. To qualify, I'd have to be virtuous as Hell.

Ha-ha. That's a funny joke.

Easy for *you* to laugh. I'm the one on trial.

Is it by jury?

Yes. If I fail, imagine my fury.

You could sue for injury.

Anything. I want to come out ahead.

Who *doesn't* want Heaven?

The Devil. He's a contrarian.

Serves him right. Let him burn in Hell.

It wouldn't hurt. He's armed to be fire-proof.

He's an arsonist. He should be in Hell.

What more do you want? He's already Hell's advocate and director. He practically *owns* the joint.

That's the kind of power I respect.

QUICK OFFER, HARD TO RESIST.

As a sexy young woman novelist, I offer to seduce you in a torrid love affair if only you, as a prominent, long established literary critic, could publish a rave review of my forthcoming novel destined to be a high-selling blockbuster.

I'm flattered by your overwhelming offer, but have to consider my integrity.

Your integrity will be rapidly overlooked once your sperm is shooting out into my body.

That sounds attractive, but aren't you in a hurry toward instant fame at an unseemly young age?

No, I'm a whirlwind prodigy. Trust me.

You look gorgeous and I can hardly resist. But my reputation as a trusted literary critic may be jeopardized by my corruption in complying with your ambitious wishes, or rather tempting offer, which could rejuvenate my dormant and rather sagging sex hormones.

Can I persuade you further? *(Lifts up her dress completely.)*

What a sight! Are you throwing money into this bargain?

No, I'm poor.

Well, no deal. I have this "thing" about money.

THE MEMORY DIALOGUE.

End-of-term rejoicing by school children used to be: "No more pencils, no more books, No more teachers' dirty looks." Ah, memories!

Are you being nostalgia's guest?

It has plenty to offer, in generous bursts and doses.

Isn't memory second-hand, compared to the original experiences?

Sure. And it even embellishes the original experiences with false and exaggerated additives.

Is memory like a cousin?

How so?

You had an experience, and then it became your cousin, once removed.

Memory is valuable enough, simply for reminding us of what once took place on a personal level.

What if it's a shared memory?

That's what builds up love and friendships.

Also resentment and hatred and jealousy.

Some memories are traumatic.

All right. Memory can be scary and frightening, gloomy, and other negative things.

Don't remind me.

Sorry. Did I evoke something horrible?

Not yet, but I'm waiting to recover.

THE IMPETUOUS PROPOSITIONING.

I can fall for a dame like you.

This seems like a sudden pick-up attempt, judging by your abrupt insolence to proposition me out of the blue, by-stepping an introduction.

Are you spontaneity-compromised?

I require orderly procedure. Convention protects me.

Risk-taking can be invigoratingly adventurous. I represent dashing romance. Take a chance!

You scare me by your impetuosity.

Aren't I handsome?

Enough so that by now you should already be snatched up in marriage and child-bearing.

I offer you that future with me.

Your improvising is alarming. I'm scared away. You seem like a sudden influx of anarchy.

I'm a wild impulse symbol. Let's run away together.

You're so dashing. My resistance is weakening.

Then you're a pushover. I withdraw my interest.

So quick?! You fool me.

Sorry I threw the wet blanket of disappointment over you.

I'm in tears.

Forgive me.

We can't go on like this.

> **FRIENDS CONVERSE.**
> **THEY DON'T REHEARSE.**
> **WHO GOES FIRST?**
> **LET HIS MOUTH BURST.**
> **HE CAN'T GET ANY WORST.**

Let's as usual converse.

Of course. Have we decided the topic?

No, it's too topical. Let's pick a subject instead.

Good. It's my turn first.

Then we reverse and I get to speak, so you'll have to listen.

Between you and me, our conversation will glisten.

First I'll have the floor.

Whatever you say, I'll be floored by your amusing content.

I hope it makes you content.

Of course, if you speak well to that extent.

I'll understand what you meant. Then my turn, with my unrehearsed text.

After you you finish, I go next.

That's the order I expect. We take our turns, back and forth.

You say your bit, then I wax forth.

Followed immediately by me.

We'll reinforce each other, to the point of glee.

Our conversation will build up to the whole world.

With you and me in it, to be unfurled.

Will it never end?

Not till one of us turns the bend.

And then the other one will apprehend.

ART CHEAT.

I just love this art museum. It's a visual treat.

But aren't some paintings considered better than others?

Of course. But you can't depend on the artist's reputation alone.

But it makes it easy on me. I don't want to go to the trouble of scrutinizing a painting carefully, just for forming an opinion of its aesthetic worth. All I need to know is: "Is he famous?" If he is, like Rembrandt or Van Gogh, I needn't bother to waste my looking-energy.

But you're cheating. You're not playing fair. If you take a good look, you've seen it, and your evaluation is fairly earned. But coasting along on the artist's reputation, you're a phony to boast how you love his work. Do you do that to impress people?

I want them to think highly of me for having good taste. I'll name-drop the famous artist's name, and then fall back on my reputation of having good taste.

But aren't you cheating yourself of visual pleasure?

It's the price I had to pay. Nothing is cheap these days. Work really pays off on people's impression of you.

But what of the work of art?

It gives me a personal message that I'm smartly well met with it.

But shouldn't you at least go out of your way?

My time is well enough taken up. Haven't you noticed modern society? It's dizzying!

So are you, you freak!

YOUNG AND OLD: FINAL DIALOGUE.

Keep life going. Once you die, you're doomed not to return.

That's easy for you, being young, to say. My death would be involuntary, I assure you. But look how old I am!

Don't admit that you're going free-fall down-hill.

How can I fight it? Mental determination is helpless against physical deterioration.

With that attitude, you're lost. I have to give you up. Should I say good-bye?

I'm still here.

But not in your "give-up" attitude.

All right. Goodbye.

But aren't you being premature? If you have an iota of life left, you have to use it sparingly. How will you spend it?

On wine and women.

Then people would think you're crazy. Wouldn't they have a point there?

The consensus of the people is the voice of democracy.

Has it come down to politics?

With political flare-ups, I'll camouflage my leaving life.

Then you'll die anonymously, in an unbroken heap.

At least I'll be among my fellow people.

You're a gregarious extrovert. That's your trouble.

Always was.

As a man of the people, are you prepared for solitude?

Now I join everyone. It's my group anti-therapy.

Are you down to your last breath? Then I must say "So long."

I pronounce it "So lung." *(Reaches death itself, feeling nothing.)*

CLOSE UP TO THE END.

Life being evidently valuable, to relinquish it would be self-destructive.

How can I hold on to it in the precarious weakness of already advanced old age?

You can't. You're doomed. How long do you have left?

Enough to try to fill my ancient head with the transferred magic of old memories from various instances of a disappearing past.

You had such a motleyed life of shreds and scraps from all over your limited map.

I can never get my memories methodically in order. They come haphazardly in unrelated junctional relays.

You re-live events?

They're my only grasp of remaining life, in desperate dispatches.

Then you're a thing of shreds and patches?

I'm lonely in my own head. I loved my wife, but death snatched her. My great old pals are dead. The wine of love and the bread of friendship vanished from my feast, even the picnic blanket itself.

You're in bad shape. I feel sorry for you. Abandoned by love and friends, how can you keep on living?

I can't. Goodbye.

Isn't that "goodbye" premature?

It's not surging, but I have a little life left.

Well, use it wisely.

That's easy. Old age is notorious for wisdom.

Yeah? I'm younger, but could you advance me some? I promise not to waste it.

Go waste it. Be my guest.

What a generous transfer!

SUDDEN CHANGE.

My wife is betraying me, loves the guy, and asks for a divorce for freedom to make him husband number two.

That's catastrophic, but do you love her? If not, just accept the divorce, be a free man, play the field, and find wife number two to marry.

That solves all my problems?

Only if you can stop valuing your unfaithful wife. Can you let her go, bystepping heartbreak?

Yes. Gladly. I relinquish her.

Good. You have a solved problem on your hands. Are you childless?

Fortunately, yes. No complications.

You're a free man. Now go your own way. I envy you. You're an unattached bachelor on the loose. Adventure ahead!

Who's my next wife?

Go to parties. That's where romance buds.

Buds, yes.

Don't be in a haste for blossoming time. Make sure future wife number two is safely in your arms.

My arms are aching with tragic emptiness suddenly inflicted.

Keep up with life's rapid pace.

First I'll mourn her loss.

Then rejoice her replacement.

How long between those sequential events?

That's the fun—finding out.

DEAD OLD FRIENDS BEING BETTER LIKED THAN AN AVAILABLE LIVE FRIEND WHO'S JEALOUS OF THE DEAD ONES.

I remember dead old friends sadly.

Well, I'm alive and am your current friend.

Yes, but I take you for granted for lacking the charisma of death as a special bouquet of glamour, the melancholy veneer of past-ness.

Well, I'm not going to die in order to oblige you.

You're easy to get, being alive. I can just phone you for an appointment. *They're* romantically inaccessible, endowed with nostalgia's profound mystery.

I'm not going to kill myself to curry favor with you. I'm jealous of the dead ones because you like them better.

Isn't it more envy than jealousy?

Oh, why quibble? In my case, it's both.

I apologize for your still being alive.

Even if that makes you like me less, I still stick to my guns.

That's the spirit. You're noble. Don't bother to hurry.

THE CLOCK'S DOUBLE LIFE.

(A) What makes a clock tick?

(B) Office workers have to get to work on time.

(A) But what happens on Saturday?

(B) Then the clock can go into idle.

(A) But it still goes on.

(B) It's too lazy to stop.

THE "CLOCK VERSUS CLOUD" DIALOGUE, DRAGGING IN THE FIRE DEPARTMENT FOR COMPARISON.

What's the difference between a clock and a cloud?

A clock has to be on time, so it hustles. But a cloud can just wander aimlessly.

It seems ambitionless, being so idle.

But it does have real emergency work to do, when alarm or alert is called upon when rain threatens. Then it has to shape up.

That's like fire department workers.

Are you up in flames? Or are you shooting your hose?

THE HARD LIFE OF A ROCK.

Does a rock have a hard life?

Not necessarily. Sometimes it just lies there.

That's too idle to make a living.

It's independently self-sufficient.

But it doesn't get anywhere.

What do you expect me to do? Pick it up and throw it?

LIFE SIMULTANEOUSLY BEING LIVED AND ANALYZED.

Life confuses me. Here I am, obviously living it. But simultaneously I'm analyzing it.

What's so strange about doing two things simultaneously?

Nothing. That's a frequent occurrence—I mean double occurrence.

Our brains have to be occupied. That's why we can't merely stop at living life, but we must analyze it simultaneously.

Or at least talk about it.
Is talking analyzing?
Not necessarily. But it's getting there.
It's on its way?
In our case, here it is.

THE SELF-PORTRAIT.

In general, isn't life wonderful?
Sure, but sometimes it stinks.
Well, you can't have it both ways.
So life is a mixed bag.
Sure. You don't know what you're gonna get.
Well, it's either fun or disappointing to find out.
You gotta roll with the punches, and grab the loot while you can.
Do you always talk in the vernacular?
Sure. I'm a man of the people. Nothing human is a stranger to me.
You take the popular approach?
That puts me in the picture.
Do you ally yourself with society in general?
Don't count me out. I'm a mass man and an individual at the same time. I'm in the crowd, but also outside.
Are you ever lonely?
Sure. But I don't always obey psychology.
But isn't psychology difficult to disobey?
Sure. But I gotta be my own man.

LOOSELY GROUNDED CONVERSATION.

If the earth is round, could people fall off?

No. Earth is so broad that its any environment is broad enough to avoid clumsy slipping.

Keeping your balance is easy?

It's an earth-bound cinch.

What about gaining weight by excessive eating? Does that put extra pressure on gravity?

Being neither Newton nor Einstein, how can I tell?

It's best to be grounded. Extra weight just makes you look fatter.

That spoils your chances for sex?

Only as a man. It might improve a woman's chances.

Don't be salacious. Roundness isn't everything.

We flatten it out to gain perspective.

Yes, those Renaissance painters illustrate that, as some museums will amply reveal.

Let's culturally see so for ourselves.

Yes. Sight is very revealing.

I could see what you mean.

THE "NOT-FALLING-OFF" DIALOGUE.

The world is round, but we walk flat, so I'm afraid.

No danger of falling off, because despite being round, the world (or globe or earth) is enormously broad. So unless you're terribly clumsy, you can walk literally miles and still keep your gravitational balance.

Thanks for the reassurance. But I'm too tired to walk that far.

COMPARING SPACE (EXCLUSIVE) AND TIME (INCLUSIVE).

Are you taking up both space and time simultaneously?

I sure am. The space I'm taking up is purely mine, so others have to keep out. It's strictly personal, only for me.

Even if you're walking around?

Even running.

Private property?

Purely.

Exclusively?

Absolutely.

How about the *time* you're taking up?

That's for everyone else in the whole world to share, simultaneously.

That's generous of you.

On the contrary, it's everyone else's property, simultaneous to mine, since they're my *contemporaries*. We all share every minute, being alive together.

It's a mutual affair?

By the billions of us.

If *that* isn't universal, what is?

In conclusion, time belongs to everyone, whereas space is confined to my personal height, width, girth.

Ever since birth?

Since conception as an embryo.

And even as a corpse occupying a bony grave?

That's going too far. Have you no sense of proportion?

FRIENDSHIP'S EXPLOITABLE OPPORTUNITY.

Why is pleasure always preferable to pain?

It feels better; whereas pain feels like something to alleviate and subsequently avoid.

That seems simplicit and elemental.

You give me no argument?

Not at all. The obvious is obvious.

End of conversation?

The subject was self-exhausting.

I agree. Why go on this way?

Because agreement is harmonious. It opens up friendship.

This is friendship's spontaneous opportunity. Let's exploit it and start it by going for a meal together.

You're on. Let's pick someplace near-by, as a convenient locational opportunity to exploit.

Exploitation is our common theme.

That needs discussing.

Sometimes exploiting is disgusting, like taking unfair advantage of someone.

Luckily, we're mutually innocent.

Let's proceed as declared.

LET'S HOLD ON.

Are you my alter-ego?

I'm not your identical life twin, but we bear mutual or alternative resemblances.

Good. I can resort to you, as a loneliness-reducer. We have references in common.

But let's not expect too much, or we lose the whole deal.

Let's not crumble apart. We keep up the connection. We had corresponding traits, but not to be worked too forcibly.

Essentially, the differences may win out. Meanwhile, let's hold on.

FATHER AND SON: PRE-PARTING DIALOGUE.

(FATHER) Life heading deathwards makes memory premium, since my past gets more relied on as nostalgic solace for what's shrinking. Goodbye the vibrant young me. Hello the feeble old replacement, hoarding more minutes.

(SON) As your athletic son, Daddy, reveling in my robust youth, I thank you for your part in birth's opportunity, and sympathize with your decline. It seems like I'm replacing you, a widower, as our family's representative on earth, for which I helplessly apologize. If your decline continues to accelerate, I'll be your orphaned survivor. I'll marry and hope to maintain generational flow into what becomes of the future....

(FATHER) Which, save in genes, I'll not attend. In advance I apologize.

(SON) Don't go, Daddy.

THE CONFUSION DIALOGUE.

If I laugh, does the world laugh with me?

No. Most of them are too far away to hear your laugh.

That's all right. I was only really smiling. I exaggerated when I said "laugh."

Well, watch your language.

I can't watch it, because I'm not reading.

Of course. This is auditory.

I can see what you mean.

NOT TAKING FRIENDSHIP FOR GRANTED.

Just because we're friends doesn't mean you should take me for granted.

No, on the contrary, I celebrate you. So if I made a statue of you, I'd make it in granite.

No, I prefer marble.

Then I'd have to make you too young, which is when kids play marbles at the gutter curb.

There ought to be a statutory limitation on your punning.

They're creative. I thought they were stunning.

THE UNSOLVED IMAGINARY POLICE MYSTERY.

Whenever I pass a policeman, or he passes me, I get scared, or at least anxious.

What's your crime, that you feel so guilty?

I'm innocent of any crime that would arouse a cop's professional interest.

Then why do you get scared, or at least anxious?

A policeman, with his badge, gun, uniform, authoritarian air, fills my imagination with my guilt, despite my having nothing actual to feel guilty about.

Is it mesmerism? Does he cast a spell on you?

Something happens, but it's intangible.

Can you define it?

"Occult" or "mystical" are too unsubstantial. Let's leave it at that.

But that begs the question.

Don't drive me crazy. Are you an undercover cop in disguise?

I'm your friend, not an officer of the law. You have some mental malady when passing or being passed by a cop. What's your problem, since you're innocent of guilt entirely, except by imagination?

My problem has become you. I stupidly confided in you, and you pester me with assinine curiosity. Desist, or I'll give myself real guilt at your annoying expense.

Don't make a police case out of it. I withdraw my meddling curiosity.

BEING POPULAR.
GOING FOR THE SOCIAL JOCULAR.
I TALK EVERYONE'S VERNACULAR
WITHOUT WEIRDLY SEEMING PECULIAR.
IF YOU THINK OTHERWISE, I CAN FOOL YER.

(A) Has your recent life gone ahead
and improved your social prospects,
so no one you meet objects
to you as a decent human being,
and gives you welcome, seeing
you as a prospective friend
worth socializing without end?

(B) I feel myself getting increasingly popular
with any number of different people,
whether atheistically inclined or to the steeple.
They invite me to dinner and even breakfast,
and don't tire of me, I'm not a pest.

(A) Is your popularity due to your smiling face
that encourages optimism in what people face?

(B) I'm simply admirable for no reason.
Guys like me never go out of season.
I never insult anyone nor commit treason.
(A) I'm won over. Can I be your friend?
(B) No. The queue is too long and will never end;
My social life is too filled up,
brimming over my over-filled cup.
Yet I allow you to invite me to sup.

LIFE'S MEANING, DEFINITION, OR ESSENCE PROVING TOO TRICKILY EVASIVE.

I have mixed feelings about life.
Join the crowd. So does everyone else.
Just what is this "life" that we're talking about?
It's too vast, variegated, and complex to describe.
Then if you find it too difficult to define life, can you at least, like a second fiddle, describe its essence?
That confounds me too.
Maybe you're too busy living life, as an involved participant and practitioner, to get a prospective perspective on it mentally.
Sounds like a cowardly excuse, a feeble cop-out.
"Essence" sounds like champagne's effervescent quintessence.
That's mere bubbly word-play, tooling with the sound of words like a board game on a rainy night for the frivolity of idle amusement's sake.
I think "life" will escape us.
That sounds like death, which is too early for us to consider in our still vital middle ages.
Let's not be literal minded. "Life" evades us as a meaning or an essence

or a metaphor for itself, but we're nowhere out of it yet in the bodily sense, so we're still safe and alive.

A narrow escape, in tricky metaphysical verbiage.

Has our conversation failed?

No. It begs further questions.

DISLOYALTY FORGIVEN.

My popularity keeps falling into disrepute. Friends abandon me, strangers look askance at me, and women reject my intimacy overtures. I'm on a losing streak that threatens, at this rate, to make me a lonely, unwanted social hermit of reluctant solitude. What do you advise?

How do I know? I'm not you.

But don't you have a modicum of empathy, sympathy, fellow-feeling?

Not in your case. It's too hopelessly repulsive. Go fight your own battles.

But I confided in you on the assumption of long-standing friendship.

I cut it short and abandon you.

Because I'm down and out, you stamp on me? You were once my loyal friend.

I'm a conformity rat. If other rats abandon your sinking ship, who am I not to follow? I go with the consensus, on the majority-rule principle.

You're a savage who smells my wounded blood and, vampire-like, sneaks your filthy snout in for the entrails as a juicy dessert.

That's a colorful description.

Thanks. I've always fancied myself a writer. Your compliment shows that, after all, you're not a bad egg.

DIALOGUE ABOUT LIFE GENERALLY AND ABOUT SOMEONE THEY KNEW IN COMMON.

Being born, following mother's and father's sex duet, is the gateway to life's double strategy of reducing pain and maximizing pleasure.

You sure said a mouthful there. You sure seem to understand what life is essentially about.

I developed that wisdom through not only being life's student, but also its active practitioner as an involved participant, as an amateur actor interpreting life's virtually impromptu scripts on time's casual or momentous stages.

What a fancy way you have of talking! Who was your writing teacher in college, if I may pardonly inquire?

Marvin Cohen.

How was he?

A high marker and generally a nice guy. The class had to shout because he was hard of hearing. He barely went to college himself.

Is he still teaching?

No; as an adjunct he was forced to quit when old age saturated him.

I met him at a few literary parties.

I don't wonder. Did he drink a lot at those parties?

Sure. He wasn't alcoholic, just cheap. It was his way of saving money, because drink was free, in addition to the free meals he managed to gobble.

Well, bless his shrewdness. I wish him well, wherever he is.

Make that double.

AN OPEN APPRECIATION.

Dear parents: Thanks for life's lovely gift. You turned general evolution's opportunity into being one life's specific benefactors: mine.

I couldn't have asked for anything better. I made something of my life, and the credit is all yours, a specific thank-you and a sealed but open kiss.

You had urgent fun in the process, briefly, but now everything is opened up for me: a slowly formed whole life from infancy through youth and maturity and all its entailings and trimmings. My days and nights, flowing through each other in alternations. All mine, in the whole world's time of generation, a part of history's spate, including my vivid contemporaries one by one, strangers and friends.

DISAPPOINTMENT IN NOT GETTING TO THE POINT.

If you want something and you continually don't get it, then you learn to give up wanting it, to reduce needless frustration in your life.

Yes, that's an automatic adjustment to save your organism from needless expenditure of hope. So what else is new?

I'm not giving you pearls of wisdom?

What you're saying is so self-evident that the very saying of it continually loses its own necessity.

When I bother saying something at all, I want to make a valid point. Otherwise it's hot air.

Good. Then resort to silence.

But silence is a vacuum in the realm of social life. Filling the air with conversation gives us a more "connectedness" feeling with other mortal human beings.

We're all in it together, as a social necessity?

Or at least try to be.

Put up pretense?

Stop pointlessness.

I see your point. But is it valid?

We try to rescue pointlessness from its obvious failure.

Failure of what?

Of making a valid point.

I know you're trying. But what's the point?

LOSING WIFE AND FRIEND IN ONE SWOOP.

I found out my wife is betraying me with a lover. Should I only complain? Or else divorce her altogether?

That's a decision for you to make. I'm merely a compassionate outsider.

Well, I'm confidentially informed that her lover happens to be you.

Coincidences are always happening, by the amplitude of time's extent.

As my friend, aren't you contrite to be my formerly hidden, now revealed, betrayer?

I feel awful. What reparations can I make?

Go ahead and continue with Jane, with my blessings, since I've taken divorce proceedings.

Can you and I maintain friendship?

Yes. But when we meet, let it be without her.

Sorry. I want her with me always, so you'll have to lose me in addition to her.

That's perfectly symmetrical. You're just as much my false friend as she is my false wife. You deserve each other.

I'm sorry it's at your double expense. But as for Jane, her ultimate transition to me will compel us to eternal gratitude.

You're welcome. No hard feelings. I've got Jane's replacement already in the gleam of my eye.

Who is she?

Ah. Stop asking.

THE STUDENT FASCIST.

I'm training to be a fascist.

At what level? Dictatorship?

Naturally.

At whose expense?

The public. They'll have to pay, suffering with deprivations, for my successful graduation into global dictatorship ranks.

Is America your victim?

Of course. That will prove my patriotism. I love my birthplace, and will make it great.

Do you plan wars?

Yes, very carefully. Not wars I can lose, but those whose losers are forced to honor and celebrate my rule as a humanitarian savior.

Is Jesus Christ your model?

No. He was too peaceful. I prefer being a ruthless barbarian, to prove my sincerity.

But isn't that bad for public relations publicity?

My charisma will countervail any adverse criticism by bleeding-heart liberals.

How will you raise armies, navies, air forces?

Through public finance. I want all the poor people to be my benefactors.

But won't you bleed the rich people too?

No. I join them and outdo them at their own game.

Well, I don't wish you success.

Then be my first torture victim. *(To guards who suddenly appear:)* Take him away. Give him the full treatment. Let his death screams pierce my happy ears.

THE STUDENT FASCIST DEMONSTRATES.

As a fascist in training, my attitude is: If you're going to rule, be tough.

But would that entail cruelty?

"You can't make an omelette without breaking eggs."

You're studying to be a cook?

No. It's a metaphor about the necessity of harsh destruction in the service of savory result. To master people, I've got to bend their will.

Are you about sheer malevolence?

That's what rulership entails: Punish their disobedience.

Whose disobedience?

Your subjects.

You mean the public? But what if they're innocently minding their own business?

It's my business, being a fascist, to redirect them with necessary coercion toward being subjects to my rulership as a junior dictator in training.

You mean interfering with their lives? That's monstrous!

Call it what you want. My fascism means to succeed.

Unfairly at others' expense?

You're slow to understand me. Finally you do.

I disapprove.

Then my henchmen are forced to persuade you.

(Henchmen appear and take over the poor sucker, while the beaming student fascist looks on in proud triumph to prove the malice of his trial case with cheerful ease.)

THE FASCIST DICTATOR AND HIS TRUSTY SECOND LIEUTENANT.

My ambition as world dictator is blocked off by inscrutable overseas complications as well as local domestic stupidity by liberal democrats with whom I'm dangerously unpopular. Have pity for our fascistic lives. Evil is a tough business.

You handsomely pay me for that pity from illegal coffers, so I'm your ever loyal Second Lieutenant.

What difficult task should I next conquerably endeavor?

The killing off of all American minority groups.

I envy Hitler, whose job was a comparative cinch.

Yeah, but he bungled it anyway by silly warfare tactics.

He was a world-class loser. I dropped him as my role model.

A wise decision. Have you replaced him with Stalin?

Don't be so old-fashioned. Television proclaims the heroic Putin.

Your modernity is consistently self-replenished.

Flattery landed your Second Lieutenant job. Don't aspire any higher.

I don't dare.

Your underdog role well becomes you. . . . Have you cleaned off my harem by executing all the over-twentyone age dollies?

I have. The remaining adolescents are clamoring for you! They have pin-up pictures of you on their perfumed walls showing your invincible cock.

I envy them for their gorgeous taste.

They've arranged a contest of who'll be your favorite.

Well, may the best young bitch win. All is fair in my democratic playground.

But the eventual losers dread their scheduled executions.

Those wretched wenches should feel privileged to die for me. But what better intellect is expected from that inferior gender?

None whatever. They're kept unschooled to cultivate their official ignorance that worships your supreme maleness.

I'll promote you some day.

THE SELF-DOUBTFUL FASCIST.

Being a Fascist is fatiguing. You always have to be in charge.

But isn't ordering people around fun? To see them cower and then meekly obey your will?

It's gratifying to my Fascistic ego. But I always have to be on the go and deal with these frightened citizens.

You wish for some privacy? Get a fellow Fascist to stand in for you, and you can be off duty. Then lie down and relax.

But my commander would wonder where I am, and track me down. The ranks of Fascism are strict.

Well, you joined it. Be proud of your calling. Fascism is a noble cause. Ruling and then ruining other people's lives can be sadistic fun.

But my personality makeup chart excludes sadism as a prime characteristic.

Then you're not right for the job?

I pray that I *am* right for it.

Prayer is illegal. Watch your step. Are you a true Fascist or not?

I'm learning atheism.

Don't let it conflict with our noble cause. I'm your compatriot, but I might blow the whistle on you to reduce your rank.

DEATH, BUT NO FAME.

Once I'm dead, what happens?

Nothing. The world goes on. It's bigger than you. The lucky live ones continue.

So without life, I'm really nothing?

That's what you are, despite what you used to be.

So I'm desperate to cling to life, at all odds?

That's the only game in town.

Does it matter if I don't get renown?

If you're not appreciated, don't frown.
If you fail, don't get down.
If barred from fame, be humble.
Be like a bee: just bumble.
Go from flower to flower.
Gather pollen, to improve the hour.
Let the thunder threaten and glower.

VERSIFICATIONS
FROM THE INBOX

HOW MISERY BECAME HAPPINESS
LIKE A BOXER'S ONE-TWO PUNCH
THAT CARRIED TO WEALTH THE BETTOR'S HUNCH.

Life is self-correcting,
depending on what you're expecting.
If you were plunged into misery,
then it's no mystery
that divine happiness was due you.
It arrived from the true blue
and swept across the scene
to make prior misery seem obscene,
not just only truly mean.
It wiped the ugly clouds away
but left a few to beautify the day.

THE TERRIBLENESS OF DEATH
BY KNOCKING OFF A SWEET HUMAN'S BREATH
AS ONLY ONE OF ITS MANY MEANS
OF DESTROYING SACRED LIFE, WHICH IT DEMEANS.

Life is so good, then why spoil it
when time gives the signal to death
to go ahead and deprive a sweet person
of her lungs' capacity for breath?
Why spoil it? For sheer perversity.
Many such incidents dot this large city.
Morality claims it's all a great pity
to kill a sweet person by means so unpretty.
But death doesn't give a damn for aesthetics
when embarked on its launch of pathetics,
like crippling the knees of great athletics.

Death is ugly and does its worst
by random killings which it hasn't rehearsed.

      WHAT TIME CAN OR CAN'T DO,
DEPENDING ON WHAT MAY OR MAY NOT HAPPEN.
        LET'S LEAVE IT TO AN OPEN CHANCE
    OF HOW OCCURRENCES OCCUR, PERCHANCE.
  MAY I HAVE YOUR COMPANY IN THE NEXT DANCE?

If you die too soon,
you'll never know what could have happened
had you had more time
to wait for a further result
of the time spent going on living
in the peculiar world of taking and giving.
Thus, time can be an enemy
of good things to happen,
by snuffing them in the bud.
But time can be a grand enabler
of what enjoyments are there, if abler.
Erratic time can be unstabler.
Any more maxims for the fabler?

        A BABY'S BIRTH MAY COINCIDE
      WITH EVOLUTION'S FINAL RIDE,
    AS OCEANS ROAR, AND THEN SUBSIDE.
      EXTINCTION DRAGS US TO THE TIDE.

Every baby is welcome to evolution
that may be on its last phase
when watery flooding numbers its days
on earth's planetary surface

that did a good job to serve us.
Every baby is a belated guest
of evolution's final ride
when the great tide sweeps us out
into random death and the empty air.
What a sordid welcome to an innocent guest
ignorant of her fate, but she does her best.
The sun sets in the sorrowful west.
The ocean's appetite is expressed
for lingering humans on a sad planet
that drowns the remains of the human race
when roaring seas increase their frenzied pace.

AN OLD MAN'S MEMORY OF LUST GONE BY. NOSTALGIA FOR SWEET IRENE RE-IGNITED THAT DOUBTFUL SCENE.

Struggling against old age's tug,
I miss the time when I could hug
a lovely woman, sweet Irene,
who hid behind a screen
when undressing into the nude;
and when sex began, turned prude,
considering an overt display to be rude:
disturbing the lust from my angry mood.
What shallow sagging
for the ardent stiffness with which I woo'ed!
This letdown stood neither of us in any good.
But she learned her lesson, as only she could.
We became well oiled, not lumps of wood,
converting the disappointing bad to the agonizing good.

A NON-DETAIL CRUISE OF TIME

The future takes its time arriving,
but makes a smashing impact when it does,
so that people surely take notice
and are changed in the same motion.
That's what time does to us.
We're the eager victims of it.
If time wears itself out,
then, in my case, it means I'm dead.
But plenty of others are there instead.
They're not me, so what do I care?
I can't function without plenty of air.
The "me" that takes in that air
has to be there and not be late.
Air and I have to directly meet
for me to absorb life's intolerable treat.
The outside world invades me,
makes me its captive so that I'm free
to just simply ponder and be.

A SURREALISTIC PORTRAIT

When life created Jacob Smullyan,
it formed him in the perfect replica of an onion
which if you peel, the tears would spread,
blinding the striving sight through the mist ahead.
Enough blinking. Then seek sweet peace in dreams at bed.

[Jacob Smullyan is the editor of the Sagging Meniscus Press, which has published several works by Marvin Cohen.]

A MAN IN A HURRY
BUT BESET BY WORRY.

When Marvin Cohen achieved birth,
he roamed about around the whole earth
and wrote about it, but his manuscript
was torn by the wind, being nondescript.
Then he spread himself out in mirth.
In tears, through literature he ripped
in wild speed, till he awkwardly tripped
and found that his zipper was unzipped.
Yet still, his sanity hadn't flipped.

TRYING TO BE WISE
IN SAMPLING A SMALL SURMISE.

Evolution allows life sexually to get born
into a baby, and then you go around the horn
seeking ecstasy to be less forlorn.
Later on you'll grow so mature,
your living nature will shatter death to endure.
Can I back up this statement? I'm not sure.

REDUCING LIFE'S MEANING
IS TOO SPARSELY DEMEANING.

To put it flighty, life "in a nutshell"
defies its own definition:
For life's sheer complexity
pounds over our perplexity,
since its aspects are too multiform
to quite narrowly conform

to an essence or core
that doesn't richly include so much more,
and further, all the other things we have in store
that if I could go over, would work me sore
and squeeze me down to my desiccated core
to wonder why I even analyze and what for.
Am I an anti-intellect kind of bore
wondering whether it was the right suit I wore?

CHANGING ATTITUDE TOWARD PARENTS WHO WERE DOOMED TO BECOME MY ONLY PHANTOMS AFTER THEY FILLED MY MIND WITH THEIR ANTHEMS.

Being born in helpless thrall
to parental mercy,
I learned to obey mother and father.
Obedience was worth all that bother.
But then the age of rebellion came,
and I was almost banned from the family name.
My parents used me as the one to blame
for all the misfortune they had to endure.
Their former infant, me, was no longer considered pure.
The tyranny of their judgment was uttered so sure.
Now it's arrived that I've outlived them,
and the fading blossom has been plucked from the stem.
Issued from my parents, what's become of me?
It's become trans-*parent* that I'm still not free.
The baby that I was, still babbles on,
but neither parent is left to realize that I won.
I'm practically weightless at this realization to stun.
Actually, I'm a father now.
That achievement had burdened my peaceful brow
to the point that even psychology doesn't allow.

Throughout the generations, I prepare my careful bow,
and adore my wife, more than just a housefrau,
who converts my lost agony into a steadier Now.

LOVE'S LIMITATIONS
THAT SOMEWHAT EXASPERATE OUR PATIENCE.

Love more than embellishes life.
But it's not a miracle giver.
It can't eliminate life's strife
nor cure the disease of the liver.
That chills us a bit with a quiver.

POETIC SELF-CRITICISM

Like the punishment fitting the crime,
I make the meaning fit the rhyme
within my mean, condensed line.
Perhaps I've crossed the line
outside tennis net and boundary?
This is enough to confound me.
The rules of the game must be obeyed,
otherwise the sporting outcome is betrayed.

DISTANCE RELATIVITY.
TAKE IT TO OR FROM THE SAME ME.

If you get too far away from something,
you'll get nearer
to being a disappearer
from what you got away from.

The closer you get to an object,
you're almost about to merge, unless you object.
Distance is very important.
If you're too far away,
distance widens and increases its distance
till you don't see it in an instance.
It's practically invisible, for instance.
East, west, south, and north
either recede us, or bring us forth.
North, south, east, and west
compete in distance. Who's the best?
North, south, west, and east—
which is reduced for being the least?
East, west, north, and south:
Are they nearer or further from my describing mouth?
—depending, of course, on "where,"
which is as close as the market will bear.
Thus I wield a compass
and feel more compos mentis
to get my bearings – exit or entrance.
I go anywhere, in my own defense.
Nor do I need to cause anyone offense.
Rather, above the fence I'll neutrally stick,
survey the whole scene, and have my pick.

I'M ONLY REMAINING

Goodbye to Jimmy Stagno forever.
We partly put our lifetimes together
from age thirteen as schoolmates
till nearly ninety when he left me
via the body fatally weakening.
What does friendship mean?

We went through it at different intersections,
now closed off. Of us, I
am the only rememberer.
A one-sided visit we do
as I represent us two
without his further contribution
in the collapsed symmetry
of grown love's sympathy.

[Marvin wrote: "Jimmy Stagno was my 75 year friend, who died recently. I dedicated 'Baseball the Beautiful' to him . . . . We were fellow Yankee fans. He was a professional minor league player till career ended by injury."]

WHO LOST WHO?

Jimmy Stagno, dead forever
after a lifetime through
of friendship ever renewed.
Only by one reviewed.

MIND VERSUS WORLD:
THE CLASH OF TITANS.
BUT THE COMPETITION UNTIGHTENS
WHEN THE WORLD FRIGHTENS
THE TIMIDITY-STRUCK MIND
TO FALL FEROCIOUSLY BEHIND.

My mind needs the world—
they clash on impact.
But the world is more compact
and draws a winning contract.

The world gives an electrical charge.
The mind reacts with its own barrage
borrowed from the instigating world.
Watch their friendship alternately unfurled
with first one in the forefront
as they take turns to confront,
and the battle sometimes gets blunt.
They seem like acrobats in a stunt.
The world outlasts the mind
whose inferiority must fall behind.
The world assumes its rightful place
but the mind somehow avoids disgrace
in underweight competition
to the world's unyielding position
renewed from along the avenue of time
to provide crucial updates, immediately prime.

MEMORY, RE-ENACTED AND EVEN PROTRACTED TO BE RETROACTIVE.

Our relation to the past is memory,
which revives many incidents
and overlooks too many others.
Repetitions of incidents reinforce recall.
Isolated incidents may be abandoned
and only re-appear at random,
unless increased by further samples,
plodding through so many examples,
that all together prove ample
to prompt part-mighty memory
to reinforce reproductive energy
and make our later years

wonderfully receptive as the past re-appears
dressed in old clothes, in its unfashionable arrears,
but welcomed anew as sweet old dears.
Let memory thrust itself forward
and mingle with *now*, even if florid.
Nostalgia is a relocated friend
intercepted from around the bend.
May its invitation never end.

I REMAIN IN MY MOTION.
THAT'S MY PRIMARY NOTION.
TO KEEP ATTRACTIVE, I DON'T SPARE THE LOTION.

If the world is considered a stage,
how badly cast is this dubious play
that features me strutting my old age?
With lots of friends and semi-friends
and even dimly lost acquaintances
being in the supporting cast,
holding on to the ship's mast
as I sail along in my only life
plying through the rugged waves,
keeping up memories that I've saved
for no occasion in particular.
I remain on an even keel
with nobody in particular holding the wheel
to steer us wherever
in whatever endeavor.
The ship takes on water but throws it off,
and like an air-o-plane it keeps aloft
during hard times but stays the course
of drifting as the waves gather
to huddle together in a conference call

to keep me afloat. I love life and all.
Welcome to the cast—friends and others.
Sailing merrily. My sisters and brothers.
I embrace you like Walt Whitman would.
It does at least myself a lot of good
in our flowing space of the neighborhood.

**IN TRIBUTE TO MY OLD FRIEND
WHOSE REMEMBRANCE CAN NEVER END
AS LONG AS I DRAW BREATH
TO CONTINUE HIS "LIFE" AFTER HIS DEATH.**

Al Lehman, where did our friendship go
when you struck me into woe
by becoming dead of disease
to grease your entry into decease?
I turned into a rememberer
and you into the one remembered,
but I was your joint companion,
so it made myself being remembered too
in lucky association with uniquely you
as our doubled lives journeyed through
all the allotted times we were able
to confide woes and joys at the same table.
Now that it's ended, was it really a fable?

[*The psychologist, Al Lehman was a great friend of Marvin's since their high school days. His name was borrowed for Marvin's novel* Inside the World, *as Al Lehman.*]

THE END OF THE LINE.
MY CONCLUSION IS THAT LIFE WAS FINE,
BUT EMBELLISHMENT NEED NO LONGER DEFINE.

Due to my ancestry, I arrived,
with my birth agony all survived,
to be the latest of my pedigree line
and take my worldly turn to try to shine,
with mother and father out of the way,
leaving the stage to be my play,
well-cast with my friends and such;
and I was given the star-struck touch.
But posterity is paying no attention
despite my ambitious intention,
so what competitively have I ever achieved?
Loyalty, because I've grieved
when dear friends croaked and died,
lone-lifying me with the receding tide.
My surviving friends are tottering
and their hobbies include aimless pottering.
With diminished prestige, no sense in posturing.
What breakthrough can pretense now be fostering?

THE LIFE SPAN,
ACCORDING TO NO PLAN.

Getting born was enough to get me through,
though mother-dependency sure did help
to get raised from when I was a whelp.
Now life and I are well acquainted,
just the way life's portrait was painted:
so authentically, it wasn't tainted.
I've reached beyond mere maturity,

having piled up seniority,
practically achieving my majority.
I'm loath to have to shuffle off.
I want to do it all over again,
but mortality stands starkly in my way
with such a growl voice, I must obey.
I'm ordered out, so I've prolonged my stay.
For all you contemporaries, "have a good day."
Soon I'll be forgotten, so that's the end of me.
Privileged was that time, when I was able to be.

MY RECORDED SOCIAL LIFE, MUSICALLY DONE ON AN UNHEARD FIFE FOR WHICH THE RECOLLECTING IS NOW RIFE.

Remembered portraits of people known,
friends foremost, then acquaintances,
down to only the briefly met,
make the social pattern set
of the population of my life
cut into tableaux or silhouettes
in time's overlapping partitions
of all my people-additions
that add to quite a collection
or a discretely assembled selection,
some by chance, and some by election,
flowing around in the odd direction
of dithering comings and goings
among circuitous to-ings and fro-ings
in a whirlwind of my recorded world
with all the objects haphazardly furled
to fly in the interstellar space

within my brain's belonging to the human race.
I'm not accountable for every last trace.

IS THE WORLD STRANGE AND MYSTERIOUS? SURE. AND WE'RE BEING PERFECTLY SERIOUS. DON'T DOUBT IT, OR YOU WEARY US.

The world that I'm a stranger to
is my own familiar world.
Is that a contradiction
as an attempt to write fiction?
No. Everything I'm used to
is weird and fantastic
if I bring my enthusiasm up to it.
Is that enthusiasm an artificial device
contriving to make something up?
Or is it just an attitude
compelling myself to gratitude
but seeming a bit forced?
Could be. But I like to pretend
and it comes true in the end.
This world is weird and fantastic
because my brain is elastically plastic.
My emotions are on notice
to just penetrate and vote us
into what's imaginarily true
as a most compelling view.
Contradict me if you will
that it's a product of my will.
But still—don't underestimate my thrill.

POLITICAL CERTITUDES
OF MATHEMATICAL EXACTITUDES
TO PREVENT REPUBLICAN PARTY FEUDS
AND STRIP THE POOR OF PRIMARY FOODS.

At an auction, an expensive painting
raises its price, creating fainting.
But all the competitors there are wealthy.
Their means to gain more wealth? Stealthy,
as long as their fat bank accounts remain healthy
and never go on a diet
due to a Communist Party riot
or a Socialist intervention
that presents poverty-prevention.
What's the next booming economics invention?
Starve the poor, enrich the rich,
and any disbeliever is a son of a bitch.

POLITICAL PLATITUDES
TO REFORM THE WRONG SORT OF ATTITUDES
AND GIVE THE DISPOSSESSED A FEW GRATITUDES.

Some say that life and politics don't mix,
claiming that it's a matter of economics
to allow the rich to take their picks
of the juicy nuggets of the stock rise
to catch poor investors in a pants-down surprise,
and all the more exalt free enterprise.
Majority rules at the voting booth
with its exacting formula: a tooth for a tooth.
Be a winner; as for a loser?
If he can afford it, he's a boozer.
As for a woman candidate? Find a way to sue her

and deprive her of necessary funds
for burying the miserable un-dones.
Make all legality illegal
under the auspice of the American eagle.
From Atlantic to Pacific wings the sea gull.
His message is plainly clear:
deprive the impoverished even of beer.

        HOW TO SANITIZE LUST
       AND CLAIM IT'S ONLY LOVE
      WHERE ANGELS SING ABOVE
     BUT NOT ABOUT ASS OR BUST
       OR WIDENING THIGHS
      AND UNZIPPED FLIES
      WHERE MODESTY DIES
        IN A GUSH OF SIGHS
      AND HECTIC CLOSED EYES
       AND BULGING SURPRISE
         ALL IN DISGUISE
       THAT IT'S REALLY LOVE
       IMMACULATELY ABOVE
     WHERE YOU PUSH AND SHOVE.

To justify lust,
say it's only just
love. Then you'll be above
mere body concern
and you won't burn
in christian hellfire
and thus expire.
Love is sweet affection
with no naughty detection
of anything at the groin

that aches to join
in a double-act
that's really love's dirty fact.
Exercise it with tact.
Be high above in a cloud
where sanitary love is allowed
to do morality proud.

A PAINFUL REMEETING AND A RATHER FORCED GREETING INCLUDING A SAD PARTING LIKE TIME WAS DEPARTING.

A former love I recently re-met
assaulted me with lonely regret
that our affair "could have been longer,"
and burst into marital song or
something along permanent lines
whose scenario shows our lives aligned.
I had loved her too, but less so,
but managed sadly to add "also,"
and we clinched into an embrace
that presented us doubly with a false face
but a tone of sincerity that we couldn't efface.
Parting, we each resumed our previous pace
but waved back in a hailing
where old love limped prevailing
with no display of outward wailing.
The years stunned us into an ailing.
Life seemed now very old
with a tone now malignantly cold.
I tottered along, my step less bold.

**TIME CROSSED ME ACCIDENTALLY
SHARED BY AN OLD LADY
UNDER MEMORY'S GLIMPSE, SHADY.
HER YOUNGER GHOST SMILED, FADE-LY.**

A woman I once long ago knew
limped old-agely into my view.
I vaguely remembered her outside shape
echoing a younger ghost in the dark
on a night when we'd both seemed to spark,
messing around under the blankets
in some unknown nowhere room
when rampant youth was early in bones
in those ancient years before cellphones.
Under her current croaking were her melodic tones,
I assumed, but beyond recall.
Somewhere near us was a deserted hall.
Today I said politely hello
in a voice that was pathetically mellow.
She couldn't hear me, having become deaf
along time's aimless corridor of theft.
Summoning a dry tear, I could have wept.
She bad me goodbye and hail farewell.
The tinkle in her voice rang an old bell.

**A NEW MAN REPLACED ME.
MY LOVE HAS EFFACED ME
ON ALL POINTS OF HER MAP
LIKE A GARTER SNAP
AND A LETHAL HEAD TAP.**

Love's reputedly fickle,
leaving a man in a pickle.

My love betrayed me
and got a superior man.
I'm left so far behind,
my ass has replaced my mind,
because my lady was unkind.
She's too happy to even mind.
Compassion? She's not the kind.
She left all apologies behind,
leaving me to mental confusion
now that she has a new infusion
with a firmer and harder protrusion.

**I LOST TO MY SUPERIOR RIVAL
AS SOON AS HIS ARRIVAL
IMPACTED MY FORMER LOVE'S MIND,
WHO PREFERRED HIM WITH WHOM TO GRIND
AND THEN LUXURIANTLY UNWIND.**

I loved her, but she's lost
to my superior rival
who, on his arrival,
made her swoon and gasp
and for him desperately grasp.
Then I knew I was in the way
and ought to shift my love life
to a better potential wife
than my old love who's abandoned me
and yanked herself away, to be free
with my most superior rival
who made an impact on his arrival,
making my former love grovel
and till his more fertile ground with her shovel,

meanwhile shoveling me out of the way
and treating me like the most common clay.

**MY SUPERIOR RIVAL BORROWED
MY ELAINE, WHILE I SORROWED,
BUT HE LET HER RETURN
TO SOMEWHAT SALVE MY BURN.
SHE HAD MY FORGIVENESS TO EARN.**

I was having a good time
enjoying my gin and lime
until the arrival
of my superior rival
who suitably inquired
as to whom I squired.
I said, "I love Elaine."
Then he made it plain
to take her away from me
and win the prestige of a key
to her intimate room
but not to be her groom,
just to be her lover,
who when he'd recover,
he'd return her to me
slightly sullied, with the same key.
Thus my superior rival
borrowed her slightly
to screw her per nightly.
I was angry when she returned,
my ego justly overturned
by my superior rival
who outclassed me in romantic survival

when he borrowed the fair Elaine
and funneled in her lane
to wield the car to have me slain
by making his intentions plain
just to toy with her a while
and conquer her with his winning smile
till the end of his borrowed mile.
Then she'd return to me,
exhausted from the loving spree
of my superior rival over me.
Would I take back Elaine
whom I'd hardly disdain?
Love made me forgive.
My wounded heart is where I live.

WHAT MY SUPERIOR RIVAL DID TO ME.
HE TOOK MY WOMAN AWAY AND MADE FREE.

My superior rival took away
the woman I most coveted
so that my heart surely bled
while he and she went on to play
with close bodies hugged together
never to part, whether
their bond ever had a future,
for he made sure to suit her
in the immediate present,
where their bodies matched so pleasant
and I was cast out in the cold
while my superior rival made bold.
At that moment I felt too old
to take on the losing role
with my superior rival on a roll

with the woman he snatched from me.
So I plucked away her younger sister
who virginally allowed me to assist her
in rivaling her older sister
for whom my sighs raised a blister
but who belonged to my superior rival
who snatched her on his arrival
in the match for romantic survival.
The younger sister I cast away,
being in love with her older sister,
with whom I could not play,
she being screwed all day
by my superior rival
since his ominous arrival
to woo and win the older sister,
assuring that I missed her
though longing to have kissed her,
whom I'd romantically prefer,
but my winning ticket did not occur.
To my superior rival I did defer,
so the ratings stood just as we were.
I termed him "an abusive cur."

MY CREDO
FOR HIGH AND LOW
IN THE LAND OF PO-
-ETRY WHERE CLIMBS THE RHYMING TREE.

Marvin Cohen is my name,
and poetry is my game.
In case I don't reach fame
and just pulled up lame,
at least I had a lot of fun

with every sort of rhyme and pun,
but I'm just not the famous one.
But how I loved poetry!
People will read it and know it's me.
My verse was perfectly wrought and free.
When I pulled it off, I was in glee.
When not, I was angry.
If you loved my verse, then thank me.
If not, then only spank me.

THE BALLAD OF RHODA.
ON OUR FIRST DATE
WE WENT FOR A SODA,
AND I TOOK HER HOME LATE.

Rhoda was my preferred love,
even mounting to adoration.
Then entered my superior rival
who immediately on arrival
snatched away my divine Rhoda,
and quickly undressing, rode her.
With expensive gifts he'd load her.
Her love for me switched to him
on an apparently momentary whim.
She was among the women
whom he aggressively collected,
packing them into a collective
called, like Mafia, "Love Incorporated."
Obviously, he found himself hated
by his inferior rival, me.
He defied conciliation
when I asked for Rhoda back.
He considered me a romantic hack

and relegated me to the back
of his easily overwhelmed pack
of notoriously inferior rivals,
all dead upon arrivals.
Being in such dreary company,
I waited for Rhoda to come back to me.
Eventually she did, quite contrite.
But we launched into a fight
over her betrayal of me
when she'd made herself too free
with my obviously superior rival
who'd too soon won her on arrival.
Will my love for Rhoda seek survival?

[Marvin says: "Rhoda is a completely made-up name & character for an imaginative, non-autobiographical amorous poem character who never existed. Irene & Rhoda & Dolores & Ruth etc. are all fictional names for my imaginative amorous or would-be amorous involvements, making me quite an adventurous lad."]

DEATH AND GRIEF FOR BOTH THE MOURNER AND HIS MOURNED ONE. DEATH SCORNS NONE, GREEDY FOR EVERYONE.

Death rouses grief
beyond belief,
so if a loved one dies
you can't believe your eyes
that can no longer see him.
Your eyes well up with tears
pondering the lost, beautiful years.

Death realizes your utmost fears.
Perhaps you're the next one
to be the vexed one,
or just be nothing at all
but a lump of bones after the fall
that hides you beyond recall
without a metaphysical clue
as what the hell happened to you.

LOSING MY LOVE TO A SUPERIOR RIVAL ON WHOSE ARRIVAL MY LOVE ABANDONS ME FOR THE ONE SHE FEELS MORE FREE IN THE COMPANY OF, FOR THE DIVINE PURPOSE OF LOVE. I'M BELOW, AND HE'S WAY ABOVE.

Love is nice if it works.
But your lady love shirks
to be in your company,
preferring that of another man
who's your superior rival.
With his arrival,
she puts immediately lipstick on
and crosses her pretty legs
as if she begs
him to fall in her lap,
and they sweetly overlap.
Where does that put you?
Out in the cage of loneliness
where it's futile to bless
her, who much prefers him
more substantially than by whim.

They shut you out, and you're grim.
Stuck without a partner,
you're forced to part from her
to leave her with the man she loves,
who's the object of your envy
and love's sworn enemy.
That's the end of me
and for him the beginning
of capitalizing his winning
(at my morose expense)
the love of your lady,
leaving you in the shady
lane of despair
to take on the toxic air.
Wouldn't you prefer nowhere?

ELEGY TO A LIFELONG PAL

Death, you've come around
to take on Jimmy Stagno, pound for pound.
Let that Brooklyn vessel lie,
with his memory's full supply,
solidly in the Long Island ground,
emptied of his baseball days.
We've come to love him, and to praise.

GOODBYE TO MY LIFELONG FRIEND.
ON A LOVING NOTE, OUR FRIENDSHIP HAD TO END.

Jimmy's out of here,
having left earth's sphere
like a long home run,

so he doesn't have to run.
His life is now officially spun
into anonymous history
clad in his open mystery.

ELEGY TO THE BEST FRIEND.
THOSE DAYS HAD TO END.
THE GAME IS OVER.
GLAD TO BE WITH YOU, OLD ROVER.

Jimmy Stagno has died.
As his best friend all lifetime,
I spied on his last years
to recognize our old fears
of that abstract horror, death,
muttered about under our breath
during our buoyant boyhood
and passionate life's afternoon.
Life was a splendid boon.
Periodically together,
we tested its various weather.
Everything survived our test
except permanent life
in which we couldn't invest.
We knew that from the onset
to hedge our frivolous bet.
Our lovely double sun has now set.
We had just about as much as we could get.

RHODA AND I WERE APART, BUT NOW CLOSENESS IS OUR ART.

Rhoda and I used to be one.
Now we're so far apart,
avoidance is considered a fine art.
Why are we so split up?
I tried to explain, but she said, "Shut up."
On our next appearance, one of us will not show up,
increasing the gap so far
that too much space will mar
proportionate distance between us.
So we'll have to join up again
and resume the kisses as before,
and blend again into our core,
while love has the courtesy to ask for more.

DISAPPOINTMENT IN LOVE REVERSES THE GLEAM ABOVE TO A SHATTERING BELOW AS A CONSTANT BLOW.

Lost love is sad to contemplate.
It means relinquishing a possible fate
of our happy marriage
and two cute cheeks in a baby carriage.
Goodbye to that old daydream
which evidently you didn't share.
We could have been an ideal pair.
But you relegated me to the offcast,
making a rotten vision of that glorious past.
Why do ideals torment when they don't last?
You've gone your way and I mine.

Between the old and the new, let me draw a stubborn line
to spare my retroactive heart
from waking up with a renewed start
of a gleaming vision with each our part.
No wonder some people abandon life and go to art.

SAD ENDING FOR ME, MAYBE GOOD FOR YOU.
I LOST MY OLD DREAM THAT SEEMED SO TRUE.

We had a date but you didn't show up
and then we lost touch.
Can we make a new date and catch up?
Oh, meanwhile you've married?
No wonder you haven't tarried
with renewed interest in me.
Alas now we'll never see
each other in possible romance.
I'll have to disperse my former trance
and give up that daydream of a chance
of you being one day my bride
to bolster up my deprived pride
and together we launch our lifetime ride.
Now I'm only recast to the side.
On that sad note I must fully abide.
I bore your image in mind.
Now I drop it and it floats behind.

**AN ENCOUNTER OF RECALLING,
TO MAKE TIME SEEM STALLING.
THE PAST YEARS WERE INDEED FALLING,
BUT TOO HONORED TO BE APPALLING.**

I saw a woman I used to know
countless years ago.
"What did we do, what were we about?"
She's hard of hearing, so I had to shout.
She only vaguely recalled
that on a drunken night we balled
and the rest was a double memory lapse
messing around and we had flaps.
It was only a momentary episode.
So in tribute I boldly strode
into her chest to deliver kisses
to atone for lost time and its misses.
She pushed me away at last,
reminding me, "All is past."
The years had rumbled on, and fast.

**THE WAY I'LL GO, MAYBE,
THE OPPOSITE END OF BEING A BABY.**

The world is pushing back at me
for growing too old,
strewing difficulty in the way
for me to give vent to play
and even harder, work,
that I have the tendency to shirk.
Living is a tired old act
and it's harder to remember any fact
or even an opinion to summon up

from all the ideas in my head.
I'm verging on the pre-dead
by amounting so many years
heading end-ward with my fears.
Wrinkles is as wrinkles appears.
My ending vaults over all those cheers.
Applause summons me to the grave
with nothing in the world I have to save,
just go as I am
and hear the barren door slam.
No curse, not even a damn.
Just my cue, and then I scram,
not even remembering who I am.

**HAVING REACHED THE END,
BENDING DOWN WITH MY NOSE ON THE FLOOR
AND REMINISCING LIFE AS AN ACHING FLAW.
UNREACHABLE ALREADY IS MY FORMER CORE.
ENTHUSIASM MELTS INTO ITS OWN BORE.**

Getting old is exhausting,
what with all the remorsing
and so much regrettable
if not already forgettable.
Old age leaves behind
my best years—"one of a kind."
Now become deaf and blind,
I'm in a foggy fix of mind,
lacking virtue, being unkind
to fellow men and women—
I come to my ultimate limit
of what time will permit.
For what am I now fit?

Just merely to brood and sit,
pondering on my loss of wit.
Plenty more too to omit.
Why don't I just quit?
Am I entirely bereft?
No, I still have spunk left
with which to fight old age
from an ever narrowing cage
that holds back my eager skeleton
all rawly naked, with nothing to put on
but merely just to reminisce upon.
I tabulate what's nearly gone
and what's left to lose,
conjuring feeble cheers and weak boos
from those recalled admirers—
old cronies and aspirers,
and earlier expirers
into the dire mist,
too faded to be missed.
Life's luscious lips I've just kissed.

UNCONVENTIONAL KILLJOY
WHO SEEKS ILLUSIONS TO "DESTROY."

When you love somebody,
is that really self-love
convincing another self-love
to combine in one great lump
and your two bodies go bump?
If I think that, am I a grump
and ought to live in a lonely dump
thinking anti-social thoughts
whose combined worth turns up naughts?

This is life's portrait, with the warts.
I'm one of those demonic sorts.

**TIME DESTROYS FRIENDSHIP
SINCE PRIVATE MEMORY IS ALL THAT'S LEFT,
FEEBLY WAGING AGAINST THE BEREFT.**

We saw each other for the last time
and our friendship vaporized to air
and installed itself in the past
where memory alone preserved it aghast.
Now the wall of memory between us
is all I have of my former friend
whose actuality had to end
when "the last time" came between
him and me like a defining screen.
The past is deposited in time
and loses itself like an unsolved crime.

**NOTHING MORE EVER
IN ALL OUR TIMES TOGETHER.
MEMORY IS SWEPT ASIDE
BUT CAN'T PUSH BACK AGAINST THE TIDE.**

Once she meant everything to me.
From out of my clutch she turned free
and now the past preserves her in air
as if she was once sitting on a chair
close in conversation with me
till only time could intervene
till it blocked us and we lost our "between."

Other reality has since passed
but "what was" is now closed up fast.
In those roles the two of us are cast.

**MY BRAIN IS ALREADY MADE UP
AND REJECTS NEW INFORMATION
AS IRRELEVANT TO ITS SET FORMATION.**

Reality is out there in the world,
speeding along to do history
and covering itself with mystery
dressed up in many facts
depicting humanity and its acts.
But my brain concocts its own opinion
based on what it's already received.
So any further outside information
from reality's field of endeavor
is rejected by my dogmatic brain
that's loaded enough and refuses to strain.
So history stops in the past
and hasn't as yet passed
into my brain's process
which refuses to consider later events
as too late to figure in my brain's concerns
which already have judged and stopped learning
even if new news buzz with active burning
so indifferent to my brain's fixed old concerning.

**NOT BEING ABLE TO CATCH UP,
YOUR BRAIN LETS REALITY PLUNGE AHEAD
AND IGNORES THE SPEEDING BULLET.
REALITY FORGES ON. YOUR BRAIN CAN'T PULL IT
AND CATCH ITS BREATHLESS BREATH,
AS SWIFT REALITY MOCKS ITS ANCIENT DEATH.**

You hear voices in your head.
Do you prefer reality instead
as truth's primary source?
Reality has got to pause
and allow your brain to take over
with its capacity to cover
more ground than reality
in sweeping up knowledge
like the archives in a college,
compiling a wisdom that's vaster
than reality's total disaster,
because new events are faster
than your brain can record,
so ineligible for the record.
Reality goes too forward,
and your brain had already stopped
when its momentum just popped.
Reality plunges too far ahead
to enter the precinct of your head,
impossible for the brain to wrap up and wed.
Too late to concoct. The world itself flies ahead.
Better for the brain to repair in bed,
linger behind the times
that do their irreparable crimes.

HAVING LIVED LIFE UP,
I SEEK THE SUBSTANCE IN AN EMPTY CUP.

In pursuit of orgasms, I go from girl to girl
and give each one of them a distinctive whirl.
Then one day my cock stopped functioning,
and instead I took to food, and went on munching.
Then I took to gambling, and went on hunching
what my number'd be, and my luck held out
till now I'm rolling in dough, from fat to stout.
The day I stop living, give me a shout
to see if I stirred. Otherwise, I'm out,
having rode to oblivion, with nothing about
and out of reach of a new telephone
whose number just creeps from zone to zone.

MAY THE GOOD STUFF STILL BE THERE
IN SMALL DOSES NOW THAT I'M NEARLY AIR.

So much good stuff in your life—
you deserved it.
But life's flight took a low dive—
you observed it.
I'm glad for the treat of being still alive—
I reserved it.
Of the time that's sorely left,
let me squeeze it—not too bereft.
Not all is stolen in the riotous theft.

CHAIN REACTIONS ON THE THEME OF LOVE AND NUMEROUS TRANSFERENCES TO HARMONY ABOVE.

A man full of self-love
and a woman full of self-love
met and sacrificed their self-loves,
transferred into one mutual love,
which they used to make a daughter whom they loved.
So the daughter grew up with self-love,
seeking a husband with self-love
with whom to make a self-love child
living in a world domestically wild.
Thus love makes the world go round
and converts it into baby-sound
that cries and bawls with self-love
deeper than the entire earth
that enjoys all this successive birth,
giving evolution a burst of mirth.

HOW TO HAVE A GOOD ATTITUDE TO LIFT YOUR SOCIAL LIFE'S LATITUDE. BUT BE SURE YOU DON'T INTRUDE AND FILM THEM IN THE NUDE.

If you're born poor, that's a bad break.
Your parents have no money to cure your ear ache,
and the only doctor they resort to is fake.
So try to reverse your bad luck

and learn discipline to earn an easy buck;
and if you marry, let her be a good fuck.
The world is an inviting place
with more potential pleasure than pain.
Increase your chances to have a goodly gain
in that fateful equation of pleasure over pain
in that wonderful city, New York,
where inviting wine awaits the tightened cork.
Getting a baby, apply to marriage with a stork.
And mind your table manners with a fork.
Let rumors circulate, but you needn't stalk
the gossip market place to rein in the talk.
And if you hear your name, don't publicly balk.
They're all a friendly bunch.
If you visit their houses, they invite you to lunch
and give you an extra full share
before, bloated, you leave your chair
and reward them with a smile, if you dare.
Thank them for all the good will they could spare
in giving you courtesy and not the air.

**LIFE'S ESCORT TO A POEM
THAT STOPPED SHORT WHILE LIFE GOES ON,
HAVING OTHER BUSINESS TO ATTEND
TO CARRY ON ITS OWN LARGER TREND
AND PURSUE EVERY PRACTICAL END.
THE POEM GETS LEFT BEHIND
WITH ITS OWN BURDEN TO GRIND.
CRITICALLY, THAT'S WHAT I'LL FIND.**

Life is going on as I write this,
and so the flow of life
gets mirrored in words after words

in comparable rhythm.
Life and words go together
in mutual accompaniment.
And so the poem is complete:
A hunk of life escorted it,
just a chunk. And here's the poem,
stopping short as life flows on.
Life dropped it off, on the way
to pursue its unpoetic daily tasks
to do what practicality asks.
It's dumped a poem, where it basks.

**THIS LOOKS LIKE DOOM,
IRONICALLY OPPOSITE MY OLD BLOOM
WHEN THINGS WERE READY TO GO ZOOM
AND AMBITION HAD PLENTY OF ROOM.**

Death ahead seems like such a lack.
My closed eyes are surrounded by black,
and the eyes themselves seem to go slack.
My outlook? I'm not heading back.

**NOT LISTED.
THIS LETDOWN LEAVES ME LISTLESS.**

Dorothy is quite a dame
and grabbed my attention
with wrenching intensity.
But she showed no propensity
to prioritize me
on her society list.
I was in the lower thousands

on her hit parade
of masculine favorites.
Such a popular dame
reduced me to shame
by no mention of my name
in her published diaries of romantic fame.

THE COMPLICATION OF DEFINITION, COMBINING A BIT OF INTUITION WITH A NON-INSTITUTIONAL KIND OF VOLITION.

The woman I love—or do I? What's "love"?
It's a compound of extra feelings,
one of which may be an old cliche-ay
so venerable, we can't get rid of it.
It's too vague, so it'll have to do
as an over-all signifyer of what love is,
which is precisely non-specific,
meaning somewhere in the vicinity of "terrific."
Is my meaning coming out clear?
That that little sweet thing is my lovely dear.

THE ME THEN, AND WHAT'S NOW. WHAT'S MY DESTINY, AND HOW.

How I became me
is an interesting study.
First I had to be,
so mother and father got together
to do the necessary act
according to their married pact.
Then little me arrived

in its infant state.
Life started to blare
and I yelled for more air.
The world was too much for me.
I was dangling but was I free?
I was in the parental grip.
But I was hungry to eat a bit,
consuming loads of milk.
Those were my concerns,
selfish and self-centered,
where my life had just entered.
Midgetly, I ventured,
and now tall here I am,
completing the arc of the span.
In between is done. Soon I scram.
In that lengthy run, I was what I am.
Time implores me soon not to give a damn.

**THE END REACHES BACK
AND SCRATCHES THE PAST'S BACK
TO RELIEVE THE EARLY ITCH
WHICH LIFE NEVER SOLVED—THE BITCH!**

My life is eking to a close.
I wear only old clothes
in loyalty to the past,
and dig up its faded blast
that went by a bit too fast
and left me puffing aghast,
tying myself to an old torn mast
while the cruel winds gather round
the last spot I'd ever be found.

MY BABY SELF AND MY NOW SELF
ARE ONLY REMOTELY RELATED
AND CAN'T BE CORRELATED
FROM OPPOSITE ENDS OF THE SPECTRUM,
BUT AT LEAST I KNOW WHERE I'M FROM,
BUT BEING APART WE BOTH FEEL DUMB.

The baby I was is now me,
having only briefly acquainted him
but too young for memory to take place,
but on faith I assume it was he
by nominal identity
that brackets us together.
I'm the baby that was,
he's the me that was not yet.
We're both part of each other,
me and my baby "brother."
Yet he was an absolute other,
too young for me, I too old for him,
and barely any meeting ground
of transitional utility,
even though life is supposed to go round,
and I to still hear his baby sound
from the tiny cradle of infantile crying.
At this end, I'm doing some real grown-up dying
which longevity is not loath from supplying.

A POET'S POVERTY-RESISTANT ATTEMPT
TO AVOID FINANCIAL CONTEMPT.

First I write a scrawl,
then I edit it
to see if it's fit

to realize all
my rhetorical standards
with show-offy abandance
to land on some Sense
to contemplate the Immense
with a Vision that's intense
to grapple with Eternity
and can also earn a fee
to pretend I'm financially free
of poverty's old ignominy
as security's constant enemy.
There's no one there to fend for me
and advance me some friendly money.

**THE EARLY AND THE LATE.
LIFE WRESTLES WITH TIME
TO SLOW IT DOWN OR SPEED IT UP
AND REFILL THE MUCH-DRAINED CUP.**

The baby that came to be me
lives dimly in supposition,
but not in literal memory.
Maybe I was imputed to be cute.
Yet now I haven't grown up to be a beaut.
People make estimates cut to suit.
The baby I once was
I assume made his little buzz,
then left off to leave the field to me
to fill in the rest of history.
How's it been? Very varied,
and full of what's contraried.
A big load I carried.
Now I'm up against impending death,

threatening to impound my entire breath.
It's a threat but I'm not worried yet.
Worrying takes too much time
that had better be used for other purposes:
to drag out and empty the surpluses
and sift out the negatives from the pluses
worthy of my remaining fusses.
My ears are ringing with these incessant buzzes.
Time's present case is compiled of many "was"es.
I wish it could all start over again but it doesn't,
or at least not yet.
Hard to collect on such a bet.
The baby and I were only briefly met.
Do I owe anything as a debt?
To both our parents perhaps?
They're dead and can't collect.
Is posthumously anything correct?

MY SUPERIOR RIVAL
VIES WITH ME FOR LOVELY RHODA
WITH GREATER PERMISSION TO BUY HER A SODA.

I vied for a mutual girlfriend's affection
with my superior rival, who owns more money
as a marital prospect,
and better handsome looks and baby-making genes,
which put him far beyond my means
for winning that luscious prize, Rhoda.
In addition, he sexually actually rode her.
Guess who lost and guess who won?
My superior rival rejected her,
having too many other women to decide among.
So by default, shouldn't Rhoda belong to me?

Not so easy. She, the sweet rejected, rejected me,
leaving Rhoda absolutely free
to pick among many other applicants
to sooth her heart for having lost my superior rival,
setting off my current arrival
at the land of old bachelorhood,
lonely and "at death's door"
with nothing but decline and decay
to characterize my sorry romantic life,
while remembering my losing strife
to my superior rival who, despite
winning the infinitely desirable Rhoda,
rejected her, having already rode her.
To whom do I dedicate this ode? Her.

I IMPROMPTU PROPOSE
TO A WOMAN JUST MET.
HOW WILL MY PROPOSAL BE MET?

When loneliness riddles my soul
with self-pity that I'm only sole,
without a verifiable mate,
insulting myself with self-hate,
I conquer shyness to aggress
at a party where I "confess"
to a lovely woman I've just met
that "my irresistibility causes me to get
marriage proposals from such ladies
as Myrtle and Gladys
and others like them,
but I just had to resist them,
awaiting you to propose to,
because now that you're within my view,

it's clear that you're meant for me
for marriage and subsequently
children to the tune of three."
But she had to inform me: "I'm not free."
I left the party and went on a weeping spree,
adding tears to my inflated self-pity.
I lost her and she was so pretty!

**MY MUSE WAS UNCOOPERATIVE
TO INSPIRE ME TO POETRY,
RESORTING TO BRIBERY
TO CONNIVE ME OF MY MONEY.
AT SUCH A HUGE SALARY,
I'D BE REDUCED TO EATING WILTED CELERY.**

I begged the Muse to inspire me
to write superior contemporary poetry.
The Muse mocked me as untalented
and threatened to abandon me for a younger poet
with a keen eye for modish fashion
as a way to harness her literary passion.
Poetry is notoriously unmarketable
which makes it all the more remarkable
that lines of poetry are on bookstore shelves
in sub-basement cellars ill-lit,
infested by squirming worms between their pages,
feasted upon by notorious bookworms
to still their ravishing hungers,
locked overnight in diseased dungeons
in sub-basements where they pack their lunches
unseen by packs of rats in bunches.
Some moth-eaten pages are floating about
in the deep dust of unnumbered illiteracy

found in bowels of this sophisticated city
where eyeglasses are worn by the book-immersed,
and critical opinions are ominously rehearsed
by ignorant scholars unlettered and inversed,
notorious for being immaculately unversed
to the point of resorting to plagiarism
to show what a plague is this whole system.

WOOING THE MUSE.
NOW SHE'S CHARGING AT AN EXORBITANT RATE
TO MAKE MY POETRY HALF-WAY GREAT.

If the Muse abandons me,
then no more poetry
issues from my pen
except now and then
in feeble spurts
of misplaced words
not belonging here or there
to breathe any poem's air
and make an earthly sense
worth more than three cents.
My Muse is playing hard to get.
She wants a substantial salary
to shine my brilliance to the gallery.

BEING AND NOT BEING
ARE TWO OPPOSITE STATES
AND I CAN NEVER GET THEM STRAIGHTS.

Life is always in the middle ground,
between what it's just barely been

and the imminent "now" about to be.
In between, of course, is merely me:
time's constant victim till I'm gone
with nothing more to dwell upon.
Consciousness is quite a gift,
setting me down after giving me a lift.
I squander life through tightness of thrift.
What's my reward for getting through it all swift?
None. I merely cease to be,
closing the case whole on "me."

WAS IT MINE?
IF IT WAS, WOULD I MIND?
LET THE MOTHER DECIDE
WHERE THE COMING INFANT WILL RIDE.
BUT I HAVE MY OWN PRIDE.

The baby waiting to get born
is from my own loins, I would have sworn,
having known the mother a while
before pregnancy warmed her smile.
I asked her, "Is it mine?"
She frowned and couldn't get decided
as to where the seed fatherly resided.
She had an idea, but she never confided
in me, a candidate,
and wouldn't even offer another date
to, despite pregnancy, possibly mate.
Paternal identity? Under internal debate.
Her enigmatic Mona Lisa smile
kept her secret, along with her private guile.
I felt insulted. Was I under trial?

MY POST-DEATH ROLE AS A GHOST
TRYING IN VAIN TO MAKE THE MOST
OF NOSTALGIA'S FUTILITY
WHILE LACKING BODILY UTILITY
AND MEMORY'S QUICKISH FACILITY.

I'm only the ghost of what I was,
storming my old haunts
to seek nostalgia's sentimentality
as compensation for the reality
that my new residence is Deathville
which hardly offers an occasional thrill
to its venerable citizens,
devoid of their witticisms,
who've outlived their stormy primes
to pursue the dusty land's grimes
in search for nostalgia's sentimentality
in the good old days before mortality
put such an end to their good old youth,
they had to choke on bones of unwelcome truth.

CONFESSIONS OF A GHOST
WHO ENDEAVORED TO MAKE THE MOST
OF HIS MIRACULOUS RETURN
TO LIFE, BUT ON A BOGUS SCALE
THAT DOESN'T LEGALIZE THE SALE
AND RENDERS ME STILL PALE.

Being born gave me a head start.
Then I let momentum do its part,
to zoom like a rocket, being propelled
through the aging sequences
until my usual defenses

against decay were shot through
and I lost perspective's immortal view.
Then I dropped stone dead
with my store of memories oozing from my head
past the deadline of bodily maintenance,
so I'm the ghostly semblance of what I was
minus the lively transactional buzz.
I haunt my old haunts
searching any sentimental nostalgia
to relieve my chronic neuralgia.
As a ghost I scare people away
and distract them from their joyful play.
I lived forever, plus today.
If you find that unbelievable,
look for your faith, if retrievable.

FROM BEGINNING TO END, LIFE WHIZZES BY, BUT SO SLOWLY, YOU HAVE TO CRY.

By birth alone we're here,
the only entrance ticket
that reality allows
by biology's permission
to complete the mission.
You start at a young age
but then the years will rage
till you claw your way to the last page
and bang!—the book snaps closed on you,
but at least you have your clothes on you
to look decent at the mourning
where your sunset eclipses the morning.

WHAT DO MEMORIES HAVE TO DO WITH SLEEP? PLENTY. THEY SHARE THE COMPANY THEY KEEP.

I remembered so much, I forgot
some things, but not the whole lot.
My life is not a complete blot.
Other people were the main subjects
of memory, which rejects
more than it can contain
of all the events that remain
lodged upstairs in my head
that I review before returning to bed
with sleepy notions to forget it all,
especially those things close to unrecall.
The unrecall shoves me into sleep
where I'm sworn not to peep
into the past so obscure,
its features temporarily must not allure
me from sleep, where I feel secure
that old memories will soon display
their buried treasures into the light of day
where they'll surely bombastically have their say,
having put aside the constraints of delay
and run rushing into exposure's open play.
That's consciousness, my plaything all day.
Then at night I repair to sleep
where forgotten memories dare not leak a peep.
They're so tired, they must quietly return to sleep,
where they work themselves into a dream
that lively turns real into what may seem
from memory's uncanny can
of worms or whatever freak monsters
interrupt the dreams with word from their sponsors.

But why make a production
that needs no introduction?

**THE EVIL RULER
WHO COULDN'T BE CRUELER.
HOW I GAINED MONARCHY
WITHOUT MAKING OF MYSELF A MONKEY
OR AN IGNORANT, BIG-EARED DONKEY.
EVERYONE IS MY FLUNKY.**

I'm the monarch of what I rule.
I didn't even have to be at school,
but naturally took over
what I discovered as a rover.
I bully the world itself
and confine it to a humble shelf
in a hidden closet out of the way
so as not to interfere with my full sway.
I work at my dominance, like play,
and colonize the lesser spheres
which I first drug to induce fears.
My domain consumes eons of years.
My rule depends on globules of terror.
I capitalize on all of human error
that leads to its own downfall,
as I romp with capacity to be all
that ever was or ever will be:
Time, memory, and history
fall neatly into place
as I romp with bully boots to outpace
the world's fraying interface
that's ripe and ready

for me to overtake
and engineeringly remake,
sneeringly in my own image
in a fight to the bloody finish.
My rule is based on who I diminish.
Those who easily lose let me be winnish.

HOW TO WIN IN THE BATTLE OF LOVE
BY AETHERIALLY PRETENDING IT'S ALL ABOVE.

To love a woman wisely,
pretend you don't, surprisely.
Pretend you forgot her name,
for which you apologize in full shame.
Then pounce on her, to complete the game.

A FAILED ATTEMPT,
BUT WITHOUT CONTEMPT.
I'M NOT EXEMPT.

I had hoped for fame,
till ambition pulled up lame,
and the public didn't know my name.
A lifetime of writing
is not relaxing, but biting,
that the world doesn't know it
although I was able to show it
via lots of publications,
not just mine, but the nation's.
They weren't picked up on
by the almighty throng.

Yet nothing was wrong.
Silent is my lifetime song.
Now death
will turn up, when it comes along
to still my relaxing breath
and annihilate sense perception
and memory reception
and philosophical conception
without exception,
since I'm not exempt
after my failed attempt.
Posthumous glory?
That's another story.

THE MATCHMAKER, WITH ME THE TAKER.

Old age is dying to introduce me to death
like a business-sharp matchmaker.
It's not for a romantic friendship.
It's strictly business: I die,
and old age has finally done its job.
My date with death is consummated,
but old age has no fee to collect.
He's left me alone with my date,
proving the match was not too late,
and withdraws delicately from our scene
played out sedately, never obscene.

DOWN TO THE END.
WILL FAME FINALLY BEND?

The public doesn't know my name,
not yet. But I'm too old
with the time running out
to make my literary clout
and win critical approval
by reviewers in prime media
to revive my career and feed her.
In novels and poetry I'm not a leader.
Will death snatch me before I succeed? Huh?
Quite likely. As for posthumous fame,
death won't know if I've become a name.

I REALLY AM WORTHY!
SO GIVE ME MY REWARD
THAT FAME AND I ARE IN ACCORD.
MAY POSTERITY THUS RECORD.

[Marvin wrote: hi Colin. another poem about literary fame urgency in the face of impending death is about to come your way in a few minutes.]

Hovering over life is death
no matter happy at the moment
your emotions rise to a summit.
Gnawing you down beneath
is a shudder to your teeth
that scary death is about to gnaw
on all your vitals, to ignore
your precious plea for fame
in the literary game,

where fame illuminates all your writing
to fulfill your ambitious writhing
and shows that your career is reviving
and your acclaim majestically rising.
Hurry, before death grabs you,
fame is riding to the rescue,
having been prompted by a previous cue
that no one's more worthy than you
and your beautiful writing
which reads so exciting.
The proof is in your books
that you're not one of the pretentious crooks.

THE WORLD IS INSIDE ME
ROOTING THERE, LIKE AN OUTSPREADING TREE.

The outside world and the inside me
should come to terms and agree,
otherwise I'm considered crazy
or accused of being lazy
about giving credit to reality
to absorb it inside my brain,
so my world is really me
with all its leaves sprouting from my tree
and taking root inside my brain,
harmonizing with my equal grain.
Altogether I can't refrain
from squeezing tight my outside world
and displaying it fully unfurled
inside my obedient brain
to both our inestimable gain.

THE ROOTER'S POINT OF VIEW

To root for the New York Yankees
is to bring out my hankies
and "cry my eyes out"
if they can't play a winning bout.
However, should they win,
my head is in a happy spin
like a ball thrown by their best pitcher
to confuse the batter. You get the picture.
That pitcher's velocity
committed an atrocity
on the enemy batter
who wrongly cried "Assault and batter!"
The pitcher's salary got fatter.

CHANGE OF NAME

The New York Yankees are my favorite team.
When they win, my face is bathed in sun-beam,
and lives the life of a living dream
where the best things be what they seem.
Ideals become their own reality
in the ninth inning after the Yankees rally
and come from behind to win the game
by a single run, to the enemy's shame.
Then how proudly I stand up to my name
as Marvin Yankee, allying myself to fame.
Or else Yankee Marvin, whose meaning is really the same.

HISTORICAL

When the New York Yankees win
a close game in the ninth inning
or even extra innings if they must,
the enemies' hopes go bust,
but my grin breaks my jaw,
creating facial surgery and more.
Now with my face all wired up,
I go and devour Yankee meat:
the corpse of the enemies they brought to defeat,
causing Yankee fans to be the elite.
They jump up from their bleacher seat
and break the wood like a lumberjack
to watch the team who from behind
rallied and more than came back:
They won the series and the Playoffs
and the World Series ever so soft
and carried the Champion banner proudly aloft
till from the heavens God Almighty politely coughed.

LOOKING BACK
AT SOME BROKEN ACTS.

I miss my old friends,
they're dead and I'm not.
I've learned to live without them,
including brief old romances
that put me in glorious trances
in the almost-transits.
I thank them for those chances.

FAREWELL, GOODBYE, AND SO FORTH, SINCE NOTHING MORE IS COMING FORTH.

When death arrives,
my consciousness will have failed,
and the brain vanished into a skeletal skull
with its power to annul
everything stored up in memory:
past, present, or contemporary.
So goodbye, it was nice to know you,
there's no more to say.
Night and day
no longer matter.
Gone is the gossip's titter-tatter.
You'll get no fatter,
nor any leaner,
you're not even an in-betweener.
Your profession? Had beener.

"THIS" IS THE SYMBOL OF "THAT" AS AN INDIRECTIONAL METAPHOR, SHIFTING WHAT I ADORE.

Love is over-sentimentalized.
You exaggerate the lady's eyes
mistaken for attributes below
that belong to her heavenly torso.
Sentiment is my boss, so
I see her eyes instead
of the foremost joints for which I'd wed
and join her on our experimental bed,
which is the reason evolution keeps us fed.

**WHAT'S IN STORE FOR YOU,
BUT DON'T LOOK NOW. HAVE FUN
NOW THAT YOUR LIFE HASN'T FINISHED ITS RUN.
AND DEATH HAS STILL YET TO STUN,
AND ERADICATE OUR FAMOUS SUN.**

Death is a serious business.
It means no more you.
Afterwards, no one describes how it was.
Heaven is a bullshit myth.
It's not there, and no one visited it anyway,
despite what the "saviors" have to say.
So before you die, expect no revelation
that you're in for an extraordinary vacation.
Expect instead a sensual deprivation
that includes all your vivacity
of your former life's capacity
reduced to passive non-activity,
not even the slightest brevity.
Your laughter's gone, and all your levity.
There's not even disciplined severity.
Everything's contrary to life's
including competition's endless strife.

**BROKEN OFF WAVELENGTHS
DUE TO ONE-SIDED STRENGTHS.**

The wonderful times I had
with people now dead
make for contrasting wavelengths.
I have the necessary strengths
to go to sufficient lengths
to still bear what we used to share.

They're so far out of the picture,
there's never any mixture
between living me and dead them.
It's even more than night-and-day,
what they can't picture but I display.
I bear the burden myself
with them all strewn on the trophy shelf
of my collection of memories
in sad, one-sided series.
My brain and their skulls
lost touch, since death annuls
their side of the bargain
by a temporarily vast margin.
Soon I'll sort of join them
in our empty-headed kingdom.
Meanwhile, I continue to sing them
if memory continues to bring them
to my ancient repetitive attention
of their dear comradely mention.

MY SUPEROR RIVAL
RUINED MY LIFE UPON ARRIVAL
AND THREATENED MY VERY SURVIVAL.

My favorite woman used to be Ruth,
and I'm telling you the absolute truth.
Our love for each other was so much,
we vowed always to be in touch.
But then who stalked upon the scene?
My Superior Rival, calm and serene.
He snatched Ruth away from me.
My misery was palpable for all to see.
Ambidextrously, tears fell from either eye,

too drenched with blur to view the sky
that collapsed on me when I lost Ruth.
My Superior Rival forged this miserable truth
upon my romantic misfortune.
He snatched her from me with the least caution
and left me nothing of Ruth for my former portion.
To get another woman, I had to submit to auction.

**HOW DEATH IS REPLENISHING ITS FATNESS
FROM LIFELONG BODIES IN THEIR FLATNESS
BY DEVOURING CORPSES' ENTRAILS,
THEN VOMITING INTO ADJOINING PAILS
TO THE SOUNDS AND WHISTLES OF YOUR WAILS
NOW THAT YOU'VE ENDED YOUR TRAVAILS
IN LIFE BY FEEDING DEATH,
TO THE LIMIT OF ITS SMELLY BREATH.**

Be cheerful in the face of death
whose teeth are nibbling on your breath.
You did all you could
in the advent
of death's showing its hand
by inviting you to its land
where your body must disband.
You tried to refuse,
but it was no use,
for death politely insisted
and discouraged your resistance
to its incessant insistence.
That's how death got you in its clutch
and thanked you very mulch
for the long life you led
that filled its belly when it fed

on the remains of you,
assorted piles of entrails
that followed the end of their trails
in a mixture of heads and tails
that went off the stomach rails,
that offered death a noble meal true
as your entry fee for its revenue,
like that of others who preceded you.
Death is so enormously fat
due to nourishment by its contributors
among its regular invited visitors
who need not be inquisitors
about their former vitals
used for death's belching recitals
after ingesting the corpses,
munching remorseless
with a certain relish and coarseness.

MY SUPERIOR RIVAL STOLE BETTY ON HIS IMPETUOUS ARRIVAL AND SANK THE CHANCES FOR MY SURVIVAL.

My love for Betty was invincible.
Of all my women, she was the principal
because she was the only one.
The planet centered on her sun.
At night the very moon
sang "Betty" in a swoon.
But then who arrived upon the scene?
My Superior Rival, stern and mean.
Right upon his arrival
was the knock-out blow for my survival
to retain my glorious Betty,

because my Superior Rival was petty
in ruining my relentless love
for Betty, Queen of All Above.
He snatched her from under my nose.
Who ever knew such ruinous foes
as my Superior Rival, who snapped my repose
and brought my affiliation with Betty to a close
by ripping her immediately out of her clothes?
Being naked, it was he she chose.
Our manly competition was never even close.
Of his superiority, I got a heavy dose.
I bowed to my Superior Rival, chief of foes
and great initiator of my romantic woes.
Betty tried to squirm away,
but couldn't find me. I was out of play.

FRIENDSHIP, ACCOMPANIED BY YANKEES. WHEN HE DIED, OUT CAME MY HANKIES.

(To Jimmy Stagno, former pro outfielder.)

Long ago I had a friend
who was with me till recently.
Then our friendship came to an end
when death came to him decently.
We loved each other back and forth
till our separation was brought
by his well-prepared-for death.
We loved each other till his last breath.
That was seventy full years,
each one worth a thousand tears.
But billions more for our cheers
of joy when the Yankees won

a great Championship, our sun
that united us for another Pennant run.
Our friendship survived a Yankee loss.
We stuck together. No one was the boss.

DOING AND KNOWING
BOTH AT ONCE:
A GREAT ALLIANCE
IN LIFE'S COMPLIANCE.

You live life, but while doing so,
think about it all the time.
This simultaneity
between acting life out
and analyzing it right through
is my life's double act.
They reinforce, not interfere,
between the act and the thought,
and they're both essentially brought
into mutually necessary play.
That's what we do and are:
in big theatre, the one star:
Behavior and intellect
elegantly bisect
as doubly elect,
bearing no discernible defect.

HOW I HELP MY WIFE
TOLERATE OUR MARRIED LIFE.

Loving my darling wife
consumes much of my life.

I need an occasional vacation
from my wife's predictable location.
So I run out to the wild outdoors
to a series of practical chores
like shopping in the grocery stores
to stabilize our kitchen needs
and stem off starvation where it breeds.
This keeps our stomachs digesting
many vitamins with every ingesting,
to keep health actively stoking
our marital harmony. I'm not joking.
Later the dishes need a lot of soaking.

DEFERRED PLEASURE
AT A LATER LEISURE
TO TAKE A BETTER MEASURE.

Leave your itch unscratched.
Thus defer your pleasure
to a later leisure
to return to the itch unmatched
by the relief of a belated scratch,
and finally release the latch.
The pleasure will be greater
when the delayed scratch is later.
Does this here finishing parable
have a moral? No, it's incomparable,
and you can call it a fable.
Leave it unread on the table.

**FOUND AND LOST IN THE SAME NIGHT.
PROMISING, BUT THEN THE BLIGHT.
A POSSIBLE ROMANCE
THAT FELL APART IN CIRCUMSTANCE.
IT WAS NEVER RENEWED, PERCHANCE,
AND I NEVER GOT TO KNOW HER TRUE EXPANSE.**

I met her in the park by the fountain
when evening was descending on a far-off mountain.
Never knew her, I "picked her up"
with a flirtational line
I pressed her to sign along to,
since maybe we shared the same view
specially unique to only us two.
She shook her head and rejected me.
Her clothes were too expensive. Mine were free
from a charity salvation shop,
and I was hungry for a lamb chop.
We came from separate financial codes,
causing our relationship to explode
and deflate that promising episode.
I was frustrated, in an unsexy mode.
But suddenly she began to flirt with me,
as her skirt revealed intriguing mystery.
We softly embraced right there on the spot,
and my cock zeroed in on her vagina dot.
But then our relationship went to pot
when I smelled too foul, as if unbathed,
so we agreed to part, unaided.
Even my memory has by now faded.
But now my body is bathed clean,
but I never re-encountered her. Fate is mean.
I could have been a king, and she my queen.

We'd get off our thrones and **** between,
on the royal marble floor
in a state mutually to adore.

A GHOST'S DUTY.
ITS PERFORMANCE IS A BEAUTY.
AT LEAST IT SUITED ME
WITH MY COMPLETE BURST OF LIBERTY.

After being dead, I became a ghost,
and that was the least and most
Death ever permitted me to be
when I had regretfully ceased to be.
To make the most out of being a ghost,
I was the hauntiest of the whole host
of ghosts who wore bed sheets
to conceal their heavenly feats
with a diversified artillery of haunting
they were not adverse to flaunting
and do their daring daunting.
I scared people out of their wits
and drove them into hysterical fits
that made them happy to soon be dead
to relieve the aches in their head.
A tomb is not a bed,
nor Death a dream
that wakes up from its violent scream
clamoring soon to be dead again
with real permanence, not now and then.
As a ghost, I did my job
to pacify the mob.

DEATH IS A CRUEL WINNER,
SADISTICALLY EMBELLISHED AS A GRINNER.
HIS CONQUESTS ARE EVER GRIMMER.

If death is your adversary
in any tussle,
he displays more muscle
and betrays your weakness
so that you speak less
and lose the physical contest
to death, who'll always best
whomever dares to oppose him
and foolishly defy his whim.
He's a winning machine
who keeps his impeccable record clean.
He's the junk king of the wreckage scene.
His attitude? Relentless and mean.
Morally speaking, he's even obscene,
with a snarl colored purple or green.
His role as an actor? He plays a fiend.
Toward that end, he's always leaned,
even from mother's milk to be weaned.

HOW THE WORLD WAS HALVED
BETWEEN LOVE AND MONEY
FOR CREDIT FOR GOING AROUND.
DID THE REFEREE'S DECISION ASTOUND?

Love boasted: "I make the world go round."
Money declared: "Pardon my interruption:
It's I who make the world go round."
Thus they fought and fought, like a boxing match,
but there was only a fifteen-round limit,

so the bout must stop there.
The referee awarded seven and a half rounds to Love,
(the result being a draw)
and the same amount to Money.
So they had to divide their honey.
They scowled at each other—non-funny.

HOW SQUIRRELS, BIRDS, AND PIGEONS LIMIT THEMSELVES TO THEIR OWN DIVISIONS AND ARRIVE AT SEPARATE INTRA-SPECIES DECISIONS.

The squirrel, the bird, and the pigeon
all keep separate lives
from each other's species
with no entangling alliances.
By keeping apart, each species survives,
allowing no inter-marriages
nor other disparages
among squirrel, bird, and pigeon
outside each'es own species.
They learn to mind their own feces
and turn their backs with indifference
to any species but their own,
and each has a separate telephone
for intra-species communication
throughout only their own nation.
Birds keep to their own tribes
and undertake their bribes
only within their common feather.
Each bird will never speak
a language beyond its own beak.
It will never spread its wing
for any non-bird kind of thing.

Squirrels only keep company
minding their own bushiness.
Pigeons only acknowledge other pigeons
and make intra-tribal decisions
with occasional parliamentary derisions
according to gradated divisions.
Birds are only for the birds;
while squirrels speak a common language
so that their proud species will not languish.
It bears no resemblance whatever to Spanish.
If you intermingle outside, you vanish.
Survival then means to be clan-ish.

[Colin wrote: I thought that pigeons were birds—am I missing something? Marvin replied: no, colin, you weren't missing something. on the contrary, I was missing something.]

TWO WITHIN ONE
IS HOW OUR DIAL IS SPUN.

Sadness alternates with happiness
within the same person.
Whose turn is it now
to wrinkle, or smooth out, his brow?
One replaces the other quick.
One's on, then it's the other's trick.
Do they feed off each other?
Happiness is the relief of sadness;
sadness the downfall of happiness
for at least a while anyway.
Let them take a mad dance together
as they change costumes in the dressing room.
Life is one long variety act

as though these opposites made a pact.
Are they reconciled? The dance over?
While one's resting, the other's a rover.
They take turns as the prime mover.
Death stills them both in the same hour,
turns off the whole general united power.
Thus wilts one sole flower
in varied nature's bunch,
for Death to make a hasty lunch,
then go on to fill his bulging belly
taking cold-cuts from the deli.

POSTHUMOUS GLORY?
AN UNLIKELY STORY.

I had sought fame
and popular acclaim
to elevate my name.
But failed, and life ran out.
Old age won the bout
with its venerable clout.
So will I get posthumous recognition
by some fortunately well-timed ignition?
Who cares? When I'm dead,
there's no glory instead
to go to my flattered head,
for me to savor.
Death does me no favor,
positively refuses to waver.
I don't even know my entombed neighbor.
Gone with me is my lifetime's labor,
so carefully piece by piece
compiled, for death totally to fleece.

You call that giving me peace?
There is no eternal ease.
A void is impotent to please.
Lively ideals have to cease.

TAKE YOUR PICK.
YOU DON'T HAVE TO BE QUICK.

Clouds and clocks don't agree.
Clocks operate where there's a fee.
Clouds are vaguely money-less,
but clocks have to closely confess.
Clouds can tolerate a mess.
A clock is definitely more *and* less
if it wants to avoid duress
or psychological distress.
A cloud relaxes easy;
a clock makes stomachs queasy.
Clouds are sloppy, even greasy,
floating along an endless sky,
without alcohol - feeling high,
letting life go just easily by
without undo concern
of what to pay and what to earn.
Clock's studious: it must learn
and be on the mark to discern.
Otherwise its precepts will burn.
Clouds love to float along,
singing stray versions of life's lovely song
that chooses itself to prolong
on the wafting stratosphere
mad at no one with a spear
and no need to cohere

to some orderly procession
based on human progression
consumed by obsession.
The cloud is without neurosis.
The clock is too phobic
to be athletically aerobic.
It sometimes even doesn't tick
any more than to shake a stick.
Cloud or clock? Take your pick.
Both earn my vote,
allowing me to equally emote.
On them then I doubly dote.
There. I've rendered my decisive quote.

[Colin wrote: so it's cirrus not cirrhosis?
Marvin wrote: I don't see cirrus or cirrhosis in what I wrote. should I have put one in?
Colin wrote: but you did!
Marvin wrote: where? what line?
Colin wrote: cirrus is a type of cloud; cirrhosis is a type of alcohol consequence.
Marvin wrote: glad I said more than I thought I did. I didn't know I had it in me. thanks for my extra full expansive extent, for which I'm glad to accept credit.]

CLOCK VERSUS CLOUD
BROADCAST ALOUD
TO MAKE COMPARISON PROUD.

Clocks are too busy to bother with clouds.
Clouds are too vaguely amorphous
to bother with clocks' compulsive precision.
Either wishes the other to rot in prison.

Clouds are components of freedom,
but clocks are responsible for commerce,
which were it to stop, they'd burst.
Clouds can perform unrehearsed.
Clocks are scrupulous about people's purse.
Clouds idle aloft,
living a life obesely soft.
Clocks have to hurry so oft,
they'd get alarmed at the slightest cough!
Their ships get snarled up at the wharf
but make sure they securely float.
Otherwise clouds would mock and gloat,
who don't care if they miss a boat
whose schedule is strictly by rote
on which they don't choose to dote,
preferring the leisurely remote
and only indecisively emote.
Which of those two merits my vote?
My choice goes to both,
and that's my decisive quote.

COLIN MYERS' EVENTFUL LIFE, FINDING SERENITY AFTER MUCH STRIFE.

As a carpenter, Colin Myers
mistook a hammer for a pair of pliers.
The construction boss then got him fired
for flummoxing the building half constructed,
having done the opposite of how instructed.
So he switched to a new field: computer science,
that enriched his previous sagging finance.
Thus he was able to retire happy,
being a slow bowler in village cricket

with an artful swerve over the wicket.
He gave up lots of runs, but he'll stick it.

*[Colin wrote that the above is particularly inaccurate.
Marvin wrote: aided by rhyming, creative fantasy overtakes life's detailed accuracy.]*

CLOUDS AND CLOCKS ARE RIVALS, BALANCING JOINT SURVIVALS IN ALTERNATE ARRIVALS.

Clocks circularly industrialize us.
Clouds can wander free
and compose fragments of poetry
without a clock-wise rhyme.
But clocks keep the essential time
for business to ring up co-ordination
and society to regulate its formation
with necessary modernizing transformation
through thorough transportational facility
and communication's electronic mobility.
Clouds pass through in nebulous arrangements,
conducting occasional weatherly changements
in the sky's neighborly attainments,
bringing awesome distance close and near
and practically taming the stratosphere.
Just to be safe, we cling to fear
and wish the rain to stop on schedule
and settle into a friendly pool
compatible with work or school.
Universal harmony makes me drool.

WHAT HAPPENING SLIPPED BY OUTSIDE MY UNOCCUPIED EYE?

How did I grow suddenly older
when I had stopped looking?
I should have maintained my watch
to not let age creep up
slowly doing hidden things
to my entire mental body
without any close study.
My surveillance had been muddy.
I didn't diligently observe
how my time chart jumped a swerve,
and there I was at that age
turning another mortal page,
confined to my chronological cage.
What happened to my alert gaze?
Suddenly I was in the next phase.

YANKEE LOVE: A BLESSING FROM ABOVE.

I love the New York Yankees.
When they lose, I weep in my hankies.
If they win, I'm over-joyed
that the enemy team has been destroyed.
The Yankees are the royalist team
and constitute my fiercest dream.
Its championship is my gleam
more than any fantasy will seem.
I'm such a New York Yankees fan,
I bear their emblem as a Yankees man.
That's pure identity, what I am.

With actual true pin-stripes,
from former agonies my heart wipes.
To lose a loss and gain a win,
my loyal heart will perennially spin
like a fish will cling to its fin.
The Yankees have owned my heart
since youth, yearning never to part.
Their baseball ability is pure art
forever, from their ancient start.
As a fan, I only do my part.
If they win, I'm terribly smart.
If they lose, convey my burial cart
and pierce my breast with a Yankee dart.
Such love conveys my poetic art.

NEW YORK POVERTY UPDATED, WITH USUAL MISERY WEIGHTED.

In New York I ride buses and subways
and pay my fare always,
especially if I get a raise
(and my boss'es honorary praise)
in my feeble salary
to buy tomatoes and celery
for my budget to excel and be free
from debt and penury.
Please commiserate with me.
I'm one of New York's poor,
a fate I must endure,
unused to wealth's lure.
ome day death shows me a door
where I get out un-alive.
My life sure didn't thrive,

stung by an entire bee hive.
And my health took a dive,
into doom and outer space.
Identity lacked a body and face
so there was nothing left of me,
even habitual poverty
in America, land of the free,
and the constitutional right to be me
if only body and face would agree
and pay a discounted fee
for the simple honor to be.

THE NEAR BRAWL BETWEEN ANTAGONISTIC GROUPS DIVIDED INTO ALIEN TROOPS WITH THE IMPACT OF A BABY CRAWL THAT RIDICULED US ALL.

Giving each other the benefit of their ignorance,
they discussed the ups and downs of finance
and other subjects of like importance,
vying to take the most dogmatic stance
and levitate dull facts into romance.
Their sentimentality appalled us,
so we decided to make, mischievous, a fuss.
Their stupidity could be detected at a glance,
so we bright people gave them no chance
to gild their brains with boasts that enhance.
We satirized them as inferior beings
and piled on the worst demeanings
to deflate their free-range bluster—
with the useless impact of a feather duster.

They rallied belligerent into a dangerous cluster.
A brawl would have been quite a spectacle.
We belittled them as unrespectable.
They countered by calling us "intellectual,"
thereby, in life's tough art, ineffectual.
In reality, they were nothing special.

REWARDING YOUR PARENTS FOR YOUR BIRTH'S TRANSPARENCE BY PAYING FOR THEIR FUNERAL, WHICH HARDLY LOOKS LIKE FUN FOR ALL IN THAT GLOOMY PUNITIVE HALL WHERE THEIR IMPACT GROWS INCREASINGLY SMALL.

Between them, mother and father
sacrificially put up bother
to produce that infant, you,
who obliged and promisingly grew
to such a bold man's estate
that now you fix up their ending state
that when they die you organize
a funeral to cut them down to size
and burden their empty heads with your goodbyes,
while in caskets the pair of them lies
innocently like their former baby and less wise.
Thus gifts reverse themselves, counterwise.
They gave to you and you return the surprise
in generational obligated compromise.

**WHAT MY WIFE DOES
TO RENEW MY LIFE'S BUZZ.
FROM HER I'M ALWAYS FUSSED
TILL WE'RE BOTH SWEPT UP WITH DUST.**

If my wife misbehaves, I forgive her with a kiss
till the next time she goes amiss.
She's lovely and I adore her
and take pains not to bore her.
All my life is for her.
Should she die, my life is taken away.
I'm too grieved to find another with whom to play.
All others lack her image
that I'm doomed to carry till my life's finish.
Her memory survives me in a breathless inch.
In death's empty brain, she revives in a pinch.
Breathe quietly on her, or I wince.
I've retrieved her always, ever since,
and in my dreams I'm called a prince.

**A NEAR MISS. MY LIFE NEARLY SLIPPED
AS MY BLOOD PRESSURE DIPPED.**

(1) My death is coming soon,
in my life's hectic afternoon.
A heart attack makes me swoon
with fatal dizziness
and a disruptive silliness
of my nervous system core,
forever never to restore.
This is a major stroke
and now I'm a weakened folk,

punctuated by a poke
all the way down my throat,
where death's early visions float
in my brain at the least remote.
Totally upset, I emote.
I can't count anything, not even by rote.
Therefore I'm doomed to drop dead.
Not so quick—it was only in the head.
I only dreamed it in my bed
with sheets disrumbled
where my balance nearly tumbled.
I'm restored to my feet,
a hardly symmetrical feat,
having lost a heartful beat.
The pillow's on the floor,
life resumes to its usual bore
with my least tolerance for any more.

(2) A quick recovery
and a happy discovery.
It was only merely a dream
making things unseemly seem.
I had a forewarning
of a premature storming
into my very vitals
from excess excitals.
I beg you—no more recitals.
(I had come to the conclusion
it was only an illusion,
causing such confusion.)

A TRIBUTE TO MY WIFE, WITH WHOM I SHARE A MARITAL LIFE WITH A REASONABLE MINIMUM OF STRIFE.

If you love your own wife,
it condenses your whole life
into systems neat and compact,
honoring love's sacred pact.
That's now a matter of fact,
determined by how we sure act.
My wife is cute and lovely.
We're stitched together, wovenly.
If I lose her, I go woefully
to my own grave and hers as one,
because our hearts are mutually won.
It's simply been a bundle of fun
to cuddle with her in the long run.
I hold her hand and kiss it.
If she were done gone, I'd terribly miss it
and only phantomly kiss it;
then request a post-life visit.
If denied, I'd insist it
and as a future memo, list it.

GIVE US A BREAK FROM CONSTANT RHAPSODY OF LOVE, DEVOUT. SOMETIMES STOMP IT OUT AND HAVE A CURSING BOUT.

Loving my wife was supposed to be consistent
with my duty, but some days I missed it,
having inadvertently skipped it.

Was that her fault or mine?
The two of us should be twine.
If that's our intention, then fine.
If we fall apart, should we squeal,
having violated our ideal?
No, give us a lapse sometime
in the love department – it's no crime.
Occasional indifference is all right
as marital slackitude. We don't fight.
We're not shined upon by the same light,
so we're each in independent dark
searching in vain for a similar spark.
When one finds one, let her say "Hark!"
for renewed love thereon to park.
Then clothes rip off and we go stark.

**AS A PARASITE,
I KEEP ON LIVING TIGHT.
CHILDLESS, IS IT MY RIGHT
TO LIVE FREE ON EVOLUTION'S MIGHT?
A FREE-LOADER, I ABIDE,
GRATEFUL FOR THE RIDE.**

Reproduction keeps on apace
to feed and frenzy the human race.
I free-loaded on the procedure
through all my hours of leisure
by giving the earth no child,
so my contribution was too mild
for evolution's cause,
causing a generational pause.
Yet ancestors combined to give me life
and heaved me into world's strife

according to the genetic code,
adding to the population load.
I even have a fixed abode.
As a parasite, I'm able to give
nothing to posterity, yet I live.
Then death passes me through the sieve.
Thank you, life, for the ride
and the chance to confide.

**A LOVELY LOVE COUPLE
ARE GOING TO GO DOUBLE
AND KEEP OUT OF MUTUAL TROUBLE.**

[Colin wrote: Maggie would love an epithalamium, if you happen to have one spare.
Marvin wrote: "I don't know what epithalamium means. Hold on and I'll look in the dictionary . . . I just did, and it means nuptial song—very appropriate. I'll try my poetic hand at it."]

Colin Myers and Maggie Beale
are turning on to the marriage wheel
which is not going to squeak or squeal.
Both have charismatic appeal.
Being together, I know what they feel.

**A LAZY BUM EXPLAINS HIS BACHELORHOOD.
HE WAS A DISGRACE TO THE NEIGHBORHOOD.
BUT STALWART, THAT'S HOW HE STOOD,
IN HIS SWORN IDENTITY AS A NO-GOOD.**

I'm a bachelor due to poverty.
Women wouldn't dare marry me,

for my job prospects were nil,
making plans for family life too ill,
with no babies likely born to me,
for joblessness made me emptily free.
Subsequent loneliness made me crazy,
but I pursued a life of being lazy.
Some women wept when they released me
from any wedding aspiration.
But I took a lifelong vacation,
and that's my sorry situation.
I'm lonely and a Bowery bum
unable to tell fingers from thumb.
My sense reactions are certifiably numb.
So marriage was not my destiny.
It would have been the death of me.
Rotten old age is all set for me,
as a future somewhat alcoholic.
I have no children with whom to frolic.
Something about my life is symbolic.

SHOULD SHE? SHOULD THEY? OH, TOO QUICK TO MAKE IMPULSE STICK.

Marrying a man on a brief short whim
makes me wonder, "Why him?"
He looked like a likely prospect,
but I didn't have time to inspect
the notion of him beyond impulse
which we both pounced upon: a momentary pulse
irrational enough to convulse.
So we drew together our heads
and popped the same mutual question:

Should we elope
and not feel like a dope?
Would we be able to cope
with unsuspected factors
and their instant detractors?
He was unknown to me
beyond this sudden meeting,
like a weird greeting,
and the spontaneity of our decision
to put ourselves in this position.
Is this our combined disposition?
It seemed like a bolt of fiction,
with us the two characters
creating the next chapters.
No, first we'd better acquaint
with each other, otherwise it's too quaint
to succumb to a rash impulse
abruptly soon to convulse
all our withholding power.
Let's not hasten the hour
of unpremeditated decision.
Let's calm down and have a vision.

THE UNSEEN POEM HAS NO APPARENT HOME TO MAKE ENTHUSIASTIC FANS FOAM.

If you try to write a poem,
put the words in the right place.
Otherwise your poem is a disgrace
and puts a curse on you,
on which the public takes "a dim view."
But the public may not receive your poem,

especially if it's not published.
Then ignore the ignorant public
who've never been exposed to you
and to whom your name's unknown
despite the author of your poem
being you personally
with definite certainty.
But what does it matter?
Your poem is an ill-written tatter
on a terrible dress or suit.
The public can't call it a beaut,
for it's beyond dispute
it's nothing, not even cute
by any critical estimation
all up and down this wide nation.
From poetry, take a vacation
into mere prose that doesn't rhyme.
Its worth is a penny, not a dime.
Even to buy it is a crime.

HEAVEN OR BUST! TO GET THERE HE MUST.

(1) Going to heaven is an unlikely event.
Yet how can you prevent
someone from actually trying?
He has to believe in deity
with an unshakable faith.
Then of course he has to die,
which is the worst part.
Can't he make heaven without dying?
At least he's dead set on trying.
Should he fail, no tears are left for crying,

since the eyes are short of supplying.

(2) Failing to get to heaven,
or succeeding perhaps.
He's one of those chaps
who has an occasional mental lapse,
confusing heaven with ladies' laps.

GEOGRAPHICAL DIFFERENCES
WITH SOME DETAILED FOR-INSTANCES.

New Yorkers are not in the heartlands.
No, sir, they have other plans.
Mysteriously by nights
they resort to what they call "Vicers Rights,"
and resort to such activities
that don't occur in other cities
(much to our concerned pities)
dotted along the heartlands,
where people openly pronounce their plans,
as long as they're not included in the condemned bans,
where people's virtues are ruined by the wrong hands
such as foreign activities in other lands.
Human nature is common wherever it stands.
Useless, then, to make other plans.

WAITING FOR HISTORY'S VERDICT?
WHAT FOOLISH NONSENSE TO PREDICT!
WHO POLICES ME AS A CONVICT
OF FINAL JUDGMENT TO BE PICKED?

The day of my death is approaching.
I've received no terminal coaching

of what to do when end will come
with year-marks on tombstone: "to" and "from,"
narrowing my history of times
to condense my chronicle of crimes
and proud boastful virtues
to allow posterity to choose
which register to emphasize
in fame's or infamy's comparative size
in competing columns that lower and rise,
when to a corpse I'm reduced
to unbreathing flesh when excused
from any fresh activity
to add to competing productivity
of columns to denote endeavors' results
according to strings of praise and insults,
when history's final judges decide
to acclaim me or to deride.
Who are these judges in whom to confide?
After all, I was only there for the ride.

COMPARISONS OF FRIENDS AND ACQUAINTANCES, SEPARATED BY FREQUENCY AND ACCUMULATION.

Memories of *friends*
had more accumulation
of memorable incidents.
But don't underrate mere *acquaintances*
who, had they more regular incidents
with you, would have racked up importance
in your life equal in value overall
to your dear sacred *friendships*
which outranked, because of accumulation,
your *acquaintances* of less frequent duration.

They all shine, the *friends* and *acquaintances*,
blessed by memory throughout the years,
reducing me to occasional tears.
Some *friendships* and *acquaintanceships* were soiled
by aberrations in smooth sailing,
causing them to end with failing.
But they don't deserve impaling.
Here then is a toast to both
before memory weakens out
and gets everything all mixed up,
so the whole jig of life gives up,
concerning those people who once turned up
or frequently, to lunch or sup
and share Robert Burns' famous cup
full of kindness and inebriation
in lives' journeys to their ultimate vacations
during the course of mixed variations.
Each person was unique in relation.
They roved about in scattered station,
subject to usual ups and downs,
mixing shiny smiles with the declining frowns.
They were all serious. They were all clowns.
(Let the Scottish vessel lie
full of poetic immortality,
though his subject was mortality,
the common theme up all of us'es alley.)

TRY TO GET IT BACK
THOUGH SOMEWHAT BEDRAGGLED NOW.
SNATCH IT JUST OFF YOUR REMEMBERING BROW.

To evoke an old memory,
re-establish its connection
to aid in detection.
What does it associate with?
What clues to reinforce
and renew its old course?
Trace it back to origin.
Find out—where did it begin?
It's yours to re-win.
Re-establish it just as born,
before unruly torn.
When you renew it, it's partly worn
since some time has elapsed
since its structure collapsed.
It's no longer original.
Time has consigned it to oblivion
(on) which you can't live long on.
Having existed, it's now gone
till memory does a hair-raising rescue
thanks to a merely passing clue.
It actually dawned upon you
in a package approximately true,
just as originally born
when experience was brand new
to being happening to you
(on the birthday faded to tombstone
if you later leave it too long).

NOT THERE ANY MORE?
BUT IT DID HAPPEN BEFORE
AS A REAL EXPERIENCE,
NOT IN MEMORY'S DISAPPEARANCE.

Memories shelter old experiences.
Sometimes memories faze out,
so the experiences drop out,
having no protection.
There's no deposit certificate
for old events that drift away,
lost because the human brain
turned frail and walks with a cane.
What happened before is lost,
sometimes at bad cost.
It's emptied out and can't be forced.
No trail left behind,
no clue for detection
or re-tracing the event
that's now been over-spent,
having lost its essence complete.
It's dissolved from the concrete.
The guardian memory can't compete.
Did the original event
receive credit?
No, it's in the debit column
which crumbles off the list,
however you may persist.
Obstinate rumor claims it didn't exist.
Never happened? Not on the map?
Too bad, old chap.

ENOUGH DEVOURING PRODUCES EXHAUSTION, WHICH WE CAN'T PUT ANY EXTRA FORCE ON.

Words get devoured by the eyes
during the process of reading.
Sperm gets devoured by the vagina
during the process of breeding.
Food gets devoured by digestion
during the process of ingestion.
Curiosity gets devoured by knowledge
during the education of going to college.
Exercise gets devoured by exhaustion
when the gasps of energy are out of proportion.
Cars get devoured by gasoline
when the speed limit is passed by Josephine.
Art is devoured by the eye
and framed for everyone to spy
in galleries and museums the world over
till legendary hell freezes over.
Love is devoured by its beautiful object
till her old husband begins to object,
and the lover of course must change the subject.
Police strategy is devoured by the suspect
who evades the law for which he has respect.
Music is devoured by the composer
whose compositions are audienced by exposure
to the ears of the human listeners.
But concert halls condemn all whispers
loud enough to ruffle whiskers.
Life energetically devours itself.
With a sigh, Death places it on the shelf.
The lungs have exhausted their breathing,
and mourning's survivors are grieving,
while the corpse was devoured by mortality

which carefully processed the fatality
in a cemetery's dispassionate equality,
serving both the poverty-stricken and the Quality
without a hint of post-burial jollity.
The tomb was clamped down solidly.

THE SUDDEN INTELLECTUAL:
HE WAS PLUCKED FROM AMONG YOU ALL.

Above you is an apple tree,
with red apples among green leaves.
You lean against the tree's trunk,
thinking idle thoughts and other junk.
Suddenly on your head an apple falls
(rather than in mid-air it stalls).
You conclude gravity is the cause,
though playing the role of scientist makes you pause.
The world's secrets are grasped in your paws,
and brilliantly you understand their laws.
"I'm an intellectual!" you declare,
throwing all doubt into thin air.
In this role you're passing fair.
You're responsible for the universe in your care.
If suddenly you had a mirror, you'd stare
and discern your reflection with awe.
You'll now research Life's inner core.
Once finding that, you'll come out for more.
What a souvenir for posterity
are the clothes you wore!
They clung to your body, and that's enough.
In your genius role, you have the right stuff,
so your chest is allowed to stick out and puff.
Your brain was previously shrunk.

Now it's discarded its native junk,
and you're no longer a moron or punk.
That apple bounced your head, and "Plunk!"
Philosopher is the role you were born for;
and university academics universally adore
you, ranked among all brains
as famously above any stains
in intellectual thinking,
devoid of strenuous affectation's conspicuous blinking.
With your unblemished mind,
you declare, "Knowledge is mine,
although admittedly it's bit of a grind.
With solitary fortitude, I'll dig and find."

IN PRAISE OF ENOUGH MONEY TO STUFF THE PREGNANT BELLY OF YOUR UNNECESSARILY HUNGRY HONEY.

The more money, the more fun and freedom.
Money is the trough that you feed from.
Money guarantees security against
inferior food lacking nourishment.
Fortify your resources against want.
Money is a great insurance policy.
Lack of money is a bitter folly
starving your capacity to be jolly.
Pile up money in the secure bank,
and your jolly existence will have much to thank,
and can even play an over-due prank
against those miserable days when life stank.

"WISH" IS LEAST, "HOPE" IS BETTER, BUT "WANT" IS BEST, TO PASS THE TEST.

A mere *hope* may get you nowhere.
But it's stronger than a *wish*, to be fair.
A *wish* is too feeble to get anywhere.
But if you want real production, try a *want*,
which comes from confidence and strength
to do the job, at any length.
So now I'll do what I *want*,
to bolster my resolve,
and any perplexities I'll solve.
So *want* can do the trick,
provided reality can co-operate,
and the situation is propitious,
with opportunity made delicious.
Temptation has to be made manifest
for execution to pass the test.
At any rate, we do our best.
From life's chances, there's gains to wrest.
When life stops, take an endless rest
and be oblivion's latest guest.

[Colin asked: but where in your clasification is 'Desire', I must enquire?

Marvin replied: desire is included within my "want" over-all compound classification.]

MEMORY?
FROM PAST ONLY,
OTHERWISE EMPTY.

Only the past is within my memory's range.
Everything else continues to be strange
that's outside of memory's focus.
Having trouble remembering? Poke us,
and dazzling days will come to life
showing how you conquered strife
and also got well again.
Memory's always in the past,
awaiting the latest blast
to renew it to the lost content.
So for the moment, be content
and enter your next event
to replenish the next memory
that you'll later recollect,
giving it due respect.
Nothing can be forgotten
unless it's previously experienced –
something happened, imperious.
Duly noted, it's now serious,
just in case you're curious.
Lost memory can make you furious.
In order to make memory official,
its source had to be experienced.
Otherwise you're merely delirienced.

HOW I EAT BETTER
BY MARRYING SOMEONE WEALTHY
WHO ENCOURAGES MY BEING HEALTHY.

Two women vied for me in marriage.
One had an elegant carriage,
the other an ungainly stoop.
But I married the latter,
for it brought me up the ladder,
having leached on her wealth
to deeply enrich my financial health,
which I wisely learned by the art of stealth.
Although my wife looked ugly,
did I make the right choice?
My bank account may rejoice.
I'm now one of the elegant boys
with an assorted luxury of the right toys.
Better than poverty, which merely destroys,
and makes for a leaner diet
that makes my power-boasting quiet,
and my hunger pangs in a stormy riot
with a thin and skimpy diet.
What deprivation! I defy it!
Better to have a full meal:
aesthetically a better deal.

POLITICAL COMMENTARY
TO PROVIDE A GLOBAL SUMMARY.
THE OUTLOOK IS NOT TOO SUMMERY
AND MAKES EVERYONE LOOK GLUMMERY.

The President in the "situation room"
plans the planet's doom.

His distinguished staff
could only laugh
at his awkward strategy
that makes a travesty
of diplomatic procedure
which creates a universal seizure
and plots wars along the globe
answering to our phob-
-ia of the world's nightmare
of too much death and subsequent scare.
What will the President next dare?

**RELIGIOUS PERSISTENCE
OF "HEAVEN'S" ETERNAL MYTH
WHICH FAITH MAKES YOU STAND WITH
TO STRIKE UP THE BAND WITH.
BUT THERE YOU'LL NEVER LAND WITH.**

Going into featureless nothing
when dying scares people out of their wits,
so that they succumb to the myth of "heaven"
as refuge from dark scary nothingness.
So they buy the idea of "heaven"
as personal deliverance from the fear of death.
But science knows that "heaven" doesn't exist,
yet scared people stubbornly persist.
Give organized religion an assist
for the persistence of that myth.
Put dollars into the church basket:
Don't you have a doubting question
but you can't ask it?
Childish nonsense, but you mask it.
Climbing "heaven" beats the casket.

Death scares the wits out of people,
so they hurry up to the steeple
on a given Sunday
to fortify themselves for a Monday
when the skies loom doubtingly grey.

A BUST.
WHAT WAS ALL THE FUSS?
DID IT COMBUST?

"Goodbye," we said to each other,
and that was the end.
What happened to me and my friend?
He was my spiritual brother,
and then the friendship dwindled
into even less than paltry little,
worth less than the weight of my spittle.
That loss divided me in riddle.
As a case, it ended in a quittal.

IT COULDN'T KEEP UP
BUT CAME TO A FULL STOP.
THUS THE PROMISE WENT "POP."

Expectation gets deflated,
then dissipated.
Was it thus fated?
Not necessarily.
Circumstance had a part
but couldn't wield its desired art.
Thus me and my friend had to part.
Broken was our glorious start.

MY LOVE WAS MY MELANCHOLY BABY.
COULD I JOCULARLY CURE HER? MAYBE.

(1) My attempts to pacify my love
to repress her anger to rise above
her deeply seated melancholy
with my pratfalls and my folly:
Pseudo attempts to be jolly.
However, she remained unchanged
the further my humor foolishly ranged.
My merry doctoring turned deranged.

(2) I had to resort to humor
to humor my angry love.
It failed to change her mood
of finding anything to brood.
Her response to my humor failed,
so repeatedly she ailed.
My attempted jokes paled
to her literal mind.
My puns were an awful grind
and excruciating beyond the point
where they could only disappoint.
I stunk up the joint
as an improvised comedian.
Next stop? Be a tragedian
and weep along with her
so that our unity wouldn't wither.
My next attempt? To kiss her
on her persistently frowning kisser.

NEVER BEEN, BUT COULD HAVE

Life is a strange place to be in.
But better there than nowhere at all,
which signifies nothing more than death.
But what if you've never drawn a breath
because would-be parents
were absent, it's apparent?
Or even one—that's enough.
Then death doesn't apply to you,
having never been exposed to a view
of an essential pre-death life,
so you had a double nullity
instead of one good fullity.
You weren't born at all,
so death didn't apply,
and you had no reason to die,
nor friends nor family to mourn you,
nor earlier parents to born you,
nor prevalent features to adorn you
and provide an identity
recognizable for plenty,
given a whole entity
bodily and facially there
for society to appreciate or bear,
or simply wiltfully stare
in the onrushing human glare,
or greet you: "Hi, there!"

TO JIMMY STAGNO: "YANKEES FOREVER."

Jimmy Stagno, known for seventy years
as my best and closest friend,

cuts me short. He disappears
into death's ordinary accident
and ruins friendship with a permanent dent
to abruptly shock the record
of venerable casual treats
and mutual enjoyable feats.
From youth to age we carried on,
and charmed was the rule we relied upon
to conversationally have a swell time
talking baseball and philosophy.
Now he's totally taken from me
and I'm only one half of what used to be.
I limp and fall with that remaining half
and pivot unsteadily on my staff.
How many times did we join in laugh?
He was briefly a professional ballplayer
and we always played together
in humble schoolyards with sticks and tennis balls.
We were serious with laughter down the halls.

**TIME TO QUIT WRITING
UPON MEDIOCRITY'S HINTING.
MY BLOODSHOT EYES ARE SQUINTING.
NOTHING'S WORTH PRINTING.**

The words look great when they're written down.
But upon review, they cause a frown.
The passionate heat of writing them
dies down and doesn't overwhelm.
What started off as inspiration
(merely copying the Muse's dictation)
turns out on further study
to indicate fame won't be my buddy.

All those years of careful writing,
now my author's status is writhing.
This is an outcome I can't be fighting.
The critics are ready with their slighting.
The reviewers are preparing their indicting.
My pile of words is not inviting.
As a writer I'm a certain failure.
Extreme impotence mangles my genitalia.
Better to leave the paper blank,
and I have cowardly restraint to thank.
Let it not be recorded my words stank
when history sums up the result
with one audacious insult.
I'm out of alternatives to consult.
Maybe I can become a fad or cult?
Or a sudden sensation
flirting with popularity's reputation
till the bubble bursts
and I come in last, not first
in literary estimates
of comparative worth,
stunning my ambitious birth
of esteem and glory
with poetry, play, or story?
I'm played out. That's all for me.

PREMATURE EXPERIMENTAL EPITAPH

When you were alive,
I loved you.
Now that you're dead,
I love you.
Your essence floats above

the permanence of my love
and floats into my soul
to revive you whole.
But not the same as you were.
The difference is: you can't stir.
Moving is impossible.
Your essence passes along
with an uninterruptible song.
It quietly whispers: "So long."

DOES LOVE GO TOO FAR?
NO. WHAT CAN IT POSSIBLY MAR?

Giving your own wife special love
is hardly too demonstrative.
Out of shyness you needn't hold back.
She's your wife, but you're no hack
to love her as a matter of fact.
It's from your own heart, not from a legal pact.
Your heart rises at her sight.
She hugs you back with both your might.
It's not competitive, so don't fight.
Mutual love qualifies as right:
Accept it, with not the least slight.

A NOVEL ADVENTURE IN READING.
TO LEAVE IT UNFINISHED YOU'LL BE PLEADING.
(A BOOK REVIEW, FOR THE LUCKY FEW.)

You start off reading a novel with alertness.
Then, one-eighth through, you bog down
and forget which characters were whom—

the ones with easy life or the ones with doom?
What was the plot adding up to?
Who was the nemesis, or the controversial one?
What parts did the minor characters play?
Was suspense falling flat? Or being built up?
Which unsuspected factor made the difference?
Where should the reader direct his attention?
And obviously what else did the author mention
to look out for, if you want to know the key
of what this elongated novel tries to be?
Is it a comedy or essentially
a tragedy no matter how you conjure it
as you ponder lost chapters while reading?
Does the style indicate parody, or straight forward?
Is it real literature, or only trash?
When did the key character go smash?
You already nodded off and fell asleep.
Did you wake up on time? Or too late?
The density of words are a mixture on your plate.
Next time read only a short story
brief enough to see the hero to glory.
The key female part was a little too gory.
But avoid at all costs a lengthy novel
so multi-faceted you need to grovel
and beg out from finishing it
before that breathless lump finishes you,
if to thine own self you want to be true.
No wonder literary critics are so few,
contemplating such a curious brew.

LOSING TO A SUPERIOR RIVAL
YOUR LOVE IN DESPERATION.
THEN HE TAKES HER ON VACATION.

When love strikes the human heart,
motivation gets a big start
to nail down the coveted object
provided, of course, she doesn't object.
Marrying her is the ultimate object,
but first a whole program of wooing
must be installed, for pursuing.
The woman objects: "What are you doing?
You're constantly bothering me, day and night,
like an obsessed madman.
However, you're not my preferred one.
That honor belongs to your Superior Rival,
who won my heart instantly on arrival.
He's lethal to your romantic survival.
I advise you to leave the field to him
to devour me obsessively, on a whim
or with betrothal's conventional intention.
To console you, we'll give you honorable mention
and allow you to attend our wedding,
providing your gift is sufficiently rewarding
in monetary terms.
So as not to infect us, it should come without germs.
Your Superior Rival and I
will then travel, we won't tell you where,
but the conveyance is by air.
Give us your gift in advance.
We'll spare the receipt, not to embarrass you
with the insinuation of distrust.
Your Superior Rival and I soon lust,

so leave us now. Fornicate we must.
He's intoxicated with my bust."

THROUGH A TELESCOPE'S LENS
TO FIND OUT WHAT HAPPENED WHENCE
AND HITHERTO WHAT WE'RE UP TO THENCE
WHETHER LEADING BRAINY LIVES OR DENSE.

Old people have to die
to make room on earth, not sky,
for a new generation of babies
to take over and prepare for maybe's
of where and how their lives will go
at the rate of grow-up speed or slow.
Chunks of real estate are re-filled up
to make bigger babies when they lunch and sup
and fill with milk their rousing cup.
The earth's available space is finite,
not easily a fly-by-night.
So old people under, and new babes on top,
are an efficient use of time and money
for mothers and fathers to replenish their honey
to take over this bold old earth
for diverse adventures since the honor of birth
provides opportunities and more
to buy and maintain this enormous store.
Earth meanwhile is the product of gravity
(while avoiding moralistic depravity)
to hold its place in the universe
to make hay to succeed (or the reverse)
with individual lives now on the re-hearse
to topple when old after filling their purse
and giving up life with a regretful curse

to have to end their days and nights
and be shoveled under after all their plights,
their battles and their grumbles and their fights.
It's extraordinary how much life excites.

BEING REJECTED BY IRENE
ENFORCED MY OUSTER FROM THE SCENE.

I wanted Irene, but never got her.
It's about time I forgot her.
She wasn't accessible,
thus I must confess so full
that my desire for Irene
from myself I should wean.
By very nature, it wasn't serene.
She didn't mean to be mean,
but had to come clean:
She wasn't the woman for me.
Thus I came adrift, and went free
as Irene's special rejectee.
She wouldn't even invite me
for a cookie-less cup of tea,
which was cold and tepid
like a lethargic leopard.

IRENE? NO.

Wanting Irene was in vain.
How could I ever explain?
Irene had no feeling for me,
so was only glad to set me free
from my over-voluntary captivity

enforced on her unwillingness.
Thus she treated me with chillingness.
The experience for me was unfulfillingness.
So Irene dropped out of my life
to end our career of strife
that hardly began to be set up
before she recommended, "Shut up!"

THE SOCIAL WAY TO GET BORN.
OTHERWISE, WHY BOTHER
IF YOU CAN'T GO ANY FARTHER
AND HAD ONLY A MIDDLE-CLASS FATHER?

We owe life to birth.
Social snobbery inquires, "Which berth,
upper or lower, as your class,
to see if your credentials pass,
to distinguish you from the mass?"
Being a baby isn't enough.
You've got to be born with the right stuff.
If you pass, then enter society
and stand out from the majority.
Be a differentialist in your piety
to distinction, of exclusive variety.
Conduct yourself with suitable propriety.
Reject your mother if she's lower class,
descended from an ignoble country lass.
For all her sweetness, she doesn't pass.
Accept your father if he's a gentleman
who belongs to the right clubs.
He's won winning tickets, and collects their stubs.
Be a discerning baby

whose blood line is on the right side of "maybe."
But go further in the alphabet than A...B.

**POETRY COMPARED WITH PROSE.
BOTH WILL ARTIFICIALLY POSE
AS MERE WORDS, I SUPPOSE.
BOTH ARE ARTIFACTS
BUT GIVE MORE THAN FACTS,
AS PER THEIR PUBLIC PACTS.**

Poetry is when you capture a feeling
in swift words that sound appealing.
Is it a matter of wheeling and dealing?
No, that's commerce.
I'm speaking about some crooked prose and verse:
Which is better and which is worse?
Words floor me. To both I'm adverse
and submit here my official curse.
Poetry is sometimes in rhyme.
Prose exchanges two nickels for a dime,
or how many lemons for a lime?
Otherwise it's considered a crime,
legally entangling you with grime,
subject to penalty in time
whether in stiff prose or dainty rhyme.
On this let lawyers ponder,
summoning crazy words from yonder.
If you produce an impossible sentence,
you're doomed to a longer sentence.
Tell me that if that makes sense.

RECTANGULAR WHITE PAPER:
"DISCHARGE YOUR BRAINS TILL THEY TAPER."

"Fill me," demands the white paper
of rectangular challenge.
"I'm blank now, but dump some words
from your cheap pen and idle brains
on me from top to bottom
in linear succession,
and have a poetic writing session.
Use of course your English language
to keep it muscular and not languish.
That's the exercise you need
to strengthen your flexible mind
to come up with the image and metaphor
that capture just what you're writing for.
The pen is full of blue or black ink.
So do let me in on what you think.
Then ask a publisher to publish it
in his available magazine
of convenient empty space,
to get judged by the public's critical face
of literacy and spleen
and wrinkled, understanding brow.
Show them what the world is, and how.
But limit it to what proportion will allow."
I take up my pen obediently
but can't quite oblige him immediately.
He's only a demanding white paper piece
to haunt me and give me no peace
till I fill it up from top to bottom
overflowing to a second page in full allot-um.

WIFE'S EXQUISITE REVENGE

I accused my wife of infidelity
(which wasn't true)
to cover up, like a coward,
my own betrayal of our marriage,
which was real and actual,
in fact perfectly factual.
My wife wept with tears
reinforced by the years
of my beastly behavior.
I hadn't acted like a savior.
As a husband I was failure.
Could I redeem myself?
I had gone too far.
She divorced me to get revenge
and put her agony to an end.
I begged her to come back
and remarry me.
She laughed and showed me her new husband,
introducing him with pride.
My shame and contrition I couldn't hide.
I'd been a beast,
to say the least.
Let her enjoy her marriage feast.
In the roster of guests, I was the least.
In fact, I was a non-invitee
and was even barred from post-lunch tea.

THE UNFINISHED POEM

The unfinished poem
by the dropped-dead poet
was his last, but he didn't know it.
The pen dropped from his hand.
Watch it, on his half-filled page, land.
But did those poetic lines span?
The forgiving critics called it "grand,"
but did that poem achieve posterity?
It led to his widow's prosperity
and added to his legacy
as a poet who died for his craft
like a sailor on a drifting raft.

ALL WINTER, NO SNOW.
THE WINDS BLEW, THOUGH,
LIKE A WAVERING BOUGH.

Spring is here; and winter's over,
but overlooked bringing snow.
Well, that's the way the winds blow.
New York City needs a blow of nature
which snow would have provided.
Winter failed to supply it,
and I missed out seeing white
thanks to winter's insolent slight.
Or was it an inadvertent oversight?
Well, we can't sue winter
for disappointing our desire.
Spring's blossoms are sometimes white,
but is that enough compensation?
No, I wanted white that was wet,

which in other winters I would get.
Expectation lost its usual bet.
But what if I run out of seasons?
I'm snow-blind with my crazy reasons.
When next winter's due,
I hope then to grovel
for reason to shovel
snow from my hovel's path
and merrily have a reason to laugh
like a cow that successfully brings a calf.

WHITENESS? WITHOUT ANY WITNESS. WE MISSED THE SNOW. NOT THE WAY TO GO.

Spring is here already.
Where was the snow of winter?
It just didn't appear.
Spring makes it too late.
All winter long I could have had it,
needing nature as a city dweller,
hoping it penetrates even my cellar.
But snow was whitewashed away
in New York history recollection,
having forgotten this year for our collection.
There should be a law
not to miss it any year.
But it didn't even come near.
Winter is the most expedient time.
But we missed it with its snowy prime.
Now we have to wait for next time
for our New York City.
Snow would have been pretty.

Missing it, what a pity!
But I guess it's not the clime
for snow and winter to always chime
in our suave New York City.
We had to bear it, gritty.
We ought to form a committee
not to bypass New York City
for deep snow to arrive,
allowing nature to survive.
We want its whiteness, live.

**THE WRONG PRESIDENT
IS OUR CURRENT RESIDENT.
DRIVE HIM OUT OF OFFICE.
HE'S THE WORST OF BOSSES.**

Our president is a tyrant.
He's an aspirant
to re-election soon.
Liberals are over the moon
to drive him out of office
so he can suck on his own orifice
and leave the public alone
with his egotistical moan
oblivious to those who groan,
as his hostility has grown
to imposed poverty.
He wants them all poorer
so his power can be surer,
directly from his sewer.
He's an illicit do-er,
and has no morals,
since hatred issues from his orals

where his mouth must spew
the confines of his malign view.
He defines what's not true
as though it were,
and makes a big blank blur,
causing a fearful public stir.
Get him out of office.
He's the worse of bosses.

HOW I GOT MY LIFE BACK AGAIN
WITH ECSTASY REMINISCENT OF BACK WHEN.

Keeping alive despite drawbacks
puts all the demons on their backs
and makes you a master comebacker
from the hackles of adversity
in New York, this biggest city.
You're life is ruined, so that's a pity,
with divorces and financial doldrums
to the bland beating of cold drums.
Your sex life has grown impotent
despite your best remedial attempt.
You were fired from all your jobs
and are reduced now to spasms of futile throbs.
Money is so much at a premium,
that a reverse mirror to see me in
reveals I'm in virtual rags,
when previously I was the connoisseur of brags.
My rating among my friends is falling,
in keeping with my life, which is appalling.
But here I am, gleaming with pride
that the Super Bowl champs are the New York Giants
on a thrilling last-minute interception

that was a serious rival to the Immaculate Conception,
unless I practice authorial deception.

THE HUMBLE ART OF PISSING,
BUT SOMETIMES YOU NEED TO HURRY UP,
UNLIKE THE LEISURELY LIFE OF A PUP.

My urine is a pale yellow
or a yellowy white,
but I'm not painting art on canvas.
I'm just indulging in harmless pissing
as innocent as Tom Sawyer going fishing.
Both equally involve fluid,
but pissing's smell can be putrid
and doesn't inspire the arrow of Cupid
unless you're being obnoxiously stupid.
If the last time you ever pissed
was a long time ago,
quick—go to the bathroom and let go.
It's not the activity of a bold hero.

THE CURRENT PLAGUE.
DO YOU HAVE AN ACHE?
LET IT BE MISLEADINGLY FAKE.

When a plague comes to haunt the populace,
it's under the category of negatively fabulous.
Keep alive as well you can;
avoid contamination
that gives all the headlines confirmation.
You and your body must fight it together
in any kind of tough weather

by social distancing and mask.
And what else? Don't ask.
And don't forget gloves,
and the uplift of usual loves.
Keep your partner company.
Or else endure plague partner-free
in stubborn solitude,
for a makeshift but inspired attitude.
You have no one with whom to feud.

[Marvin added:
The plague's the thing
That captures the guilt of the king.]

FROM THE INFANT'S VIEWPOINT.
HE'S ABLE TO SHOUT AND POINT.

Being born, you're too dumb to welcome it
as an opportunity to grow up and live,
being tiny and barely alive,
craving mom's milk to guzzle and thrive.
Being grateful to parents is too early.
They appear rather grumpy and surly.
Exploit mother and father both
for honoring responsibility
for your decent upbringing
despite relative poverty.
Being infantile, you're lingering
to decipher what the future is bringing.
But ignorant innocence prevents
my parents' verbal tones to make sense.
They argue something fierce and intense,
maybe at my expense.

Please honor me, mom and pop:
I'm your first fertile crop.
Now you have permission to stop
screwing for reproduction,
since I'm your major production.

PROBLEMS SOLVED
BY PROVING MYSELF RESOLVED.

I had a bout of insomnia,
but thought better to sleep it off,
which proved to be a curative process.
I woke up bright, happy with progress.
The moral of this bedtime story
is to go right into the heart of the problem.
Insomnia, which stops sleep,
enlists the help of urination
to interrupt the said sleep.
Back to bed after urination,
I fell back to sleep again
and had my insomnia licked
when much restored, I woke up and kicked
the blanket off the bed,
then resolved to get myself well fed.

SOME NOTES ON DEATH,
WITH ITS REPUTATION FOR BEING DREAD.
FOR GOOD REASON:
ITS VICTIMS ARE DEAD.

Death, by any other name,
is just as grim.

Is it a "her" or a "him"?
Neither. It lacks gender,
and is not known for being tender.
It's actually sexless
or only a neuter.
If it's a woman, it lacks a suitor.
If it's a man, it's brazen like pewter.
I looked it up on my computer.
Anyone refuting death is a deluder.
It snares you so quick, like a burgular looter.
Beware the ravages of death.
It wipes you clean through, not only breath.
It lives up to its horrid name
and deserves its insufferable fame.

FROM PARTY TO DYNASTY, ENLARGING YOUR LOVE FINALLY.

When something is wrong, right it,
which if not easy, then fight it.
Every problem admits of a solution,
so clean up all pollution,
and balance out what's awry;
so if you're lonely, find someone to mate with.
Doomed to be solitary? That's a myth.
You'll find your true love at a party.
Look carefully, there she is.
Courageously accost her.
What will it cost you?
Trouble to put timidity away
and boldly introduce yourself,
like you're a conquering hero,
while inwardly you tremble like a zero.

The party's alcohol will give you courage.
If at first she appears indifferent,
make a scene to capture her interest.
Winning her love will be a big gain
in your life, so ask her to wed you.
After going out on an exploratory date,
you spring the question to open the gate
to matrimony's combined old bliss.
Sort your clothes between "hers" and "his"
in your new flat, and wait for a baby
to crown successful love without a maybe.
Maybe you'll start a whole dynasty
of family conjugation.
Let the bed be your launching station.
The human race benefits by this creation
by swelling its whole population
thanks originally to a party's invitation;
or maybe you crashed it?
You had the address and flashed it.

MEMORY LOSS
IS MY NEW BOSS.

Struggle against memory loss
makes forgetfulness my boss,
documents my old age,
and rips words off the page
in which I've just engaged.
Words disappear out of my mind,
and I've even lost the paper I've signed.
If this goes on, I will have lost my mind
that I searched the whole body below to find.
My brain to me has not remained kind.

I forgot which kind of brain I had
before the whole brain started to go bad.
When was it that led me to be sad?
I hope I don't lose money out of my wad.
Finding it is another thing.
What relief it will bring!
No bird should ever lose its left or right wing.
Flying by then has gone off the wring,
and the poor bird has to pay for his own bill
with which he snatched food. What a thrill
to do the deed with determined will!
However, its ability has gone still
with no new errand to fill.
I remember things by rhyme:
Two nickels for a dime.
Forget it? Too unkind,
I must be losing my mind.
I never thought I'd be the kind.
A rhyme keeps me sane.
Isn't that by now plain?

WILDLIFE AND PEOPLE TOO
COMPRISE NEW YORK'S WANDERING ZOO.

Squirrels, cute birds, and pigeons
(and don't forget, dogs and cats,
who are less wildlife but domesticated)
occupy Manhattan's wandering zoo
helter-skelter on land or ground,
and scamper up trees,
and fly to the top.
Human beings throng in their midst,
giving noisy traffic an assist.

We all get along fine.
They're decorative and hardly annoy.
Everyone has business to do,
single-minded, in this wandering zoo.
Those who are disencumbered are few.
People walk or ride to work.
Their set duties they hardly shirk.
Little ones of respective species
are gotten food for,
by concentration on the work at hand
by this disorganized but orderly band
in this limited but universal land.
Ignoring each other is ordinarily grand.
A dull color keeps things vividly bland.
The city is united by routine,
unlike the country that's traditionally green.

DEATH AND LOVE
ARE A WEIRD COMBINATION
TO SUSTAIN IN ALTERNATION.

Candace Watt is my lovely wife.
Occasionally we have spasms of strife.
She's learning to walk again.
The constant home-health aids are expensive.
I love her more and more
as the past recedes and the future looms,
and all the dust is swept with brooms.
Let's live and die together;
she's my future and my past.
How long will we last?

[Candace says: "she was born in Connecticut and after college she moved to New York where she was an editor in book publishing. She first met Marvin at a dinner party and they married in 1986.]

**LET'S OPPOSE DEATH
WITH OUR ALTERNATE RHYTHM OF BREATH.**

Death is a frightening prospect
so far as anyone can detect.
Life is more precious loving Candace Watt,
but now the two of us are on the spot.
Let's struggle to live longer,
because my love is already much stronger.

**RETURNING A COMPLIMENT
EASY AS A CANDY CONDIMENT
SWALLOWED LIKE IT'S SURELY MEANT
IN A DELICIOUS INTENT
ACCORDING TO OUR TASTE'S BENT.**

Loving Candace Watt
is like connecting every dot
without making a blot.
I ask her what
her charm is due to,
but she only proclaims, "You too!"

HOW POETS LIVE.
WHAT WE MUST GIVE
TO PRESERVE THEIR PRECIOUS GIFT
TO GIVE US SPIRITUAL UPLIFT.

Poets are like ordinary men
like how they react to a woman:
They ask her, "Let's go for a swim
to see if your bathing suit is in good trim."
If you ask a poet about money,
he asks, "How high must you pay for bees' honey?
If you ask too low, then you've been stung
when what you receive is a carton of dung."
But poets are actually realistic
and examine the latest stock market statistic,
which if too low, they retch and are sick.
Poets are just like the rest of us:
They won't let adversaries get the best of us.
Poets even go to sporting events,
but confuse the visiting team's dugout for tents
that open out to reveal a slugger
who beats you with a home run like a bugger.
Anyway, treat poets all right.
They're alert, and don't confuse day from night.
And if a danger approaches, they take fright.
They return home to write a rhyme,
unless for free verse it's just about time
to loosen up and feel free
like the rest of us: you and me.

**WHAT LUCK I HAD!
DEATH AVOIDED ME. THAT'S NOT BAD.
I WAS INDEED A LUCKY LAD
TO BE SO INCREDIBLY SPARED.**

Somehow I avoided death
and retained my essential breath.
This made me so unique,
I must be an immortal freak.
I managed my precious life to keep.
Between worlds, what a leap!
Death had overlooked me.
What a crook I must be!
Would I have to pay redemption?
Or would I continue as a lucky exemption
to avoid the usual execution?
What problem led to this solution
that everybody died except me?
All were ensnared; I remained free.
Why was my destiny so exceptional
down to the last decimal?
Was it just luck? Or what?
I can't seem to connect that dot
to all the rest of the lot.
Maybe it was an eternal plot?
I must avoid conspiracy theory.
It makes the world of politics so weary.
From that solution I remain leery.
Yet the problem still remains.
How did I steer clear of Death's stains?
Maybe my skull had some extra brains?
Maybe my breakfast cereal had unique grains?
How shocking that in my case Death refrains!
Nothing in normal life explains.

TIME'S LIABILITY WITH NO ABILITY TO LIE.

When I was young and handsome
though also slightly dumb,
women were attracted to me.
Later on, it's not to be.
Women side-step when I'm in their way.
Their instinct is not to play
with an old man who wastes their time
with ineffectual flirting, that crime
imposed on me by the length of time
it takes to get too old
to in your arms strange women fold.
I just don't fit the modern mold.
"Lay off!" I'm told,
not too delicately put.
I could swallow my mouth with my foot.

A SLIGHT NUDGE

I've gotten dangerously old,
and death's fear is upon me.
I want to live the usual way,
mixing writing with idle play.
But death slithers along my side
and edges my bone-thin backside
with a slight nudge, as if to say,
"Isn't it time now to call it a day?
I'll visit you soon now, if I may."
That creepy nudge I'll surely feel
till death turns its automatic wheel.

AN ODE TO WORDS

Death shuts your mouth up
with permanent stoppage.
You who were so loquacious,
you made everyone else vivacious!
Words were your social medium
to cure all silent tedium.
Words filled up the vacuum
so that you can breathe and exhume
and give yourself some open room
to shore up defense against doom
that silently paused itself to loom.

STORY OF MY LIFE, TRYING TO SOFTEN STRIFE.

I thanked evolution for making me exist
and being able on my own to persist.
I didn't ask to be alive,
but here I am, so I try to thrive.
Mostly all I've done is survive.
I love friendship and love,
and dread being a subjective hermit.
I'm here in life without permit.
The world is a wide and gregarious place,
where I try to find a nook.
Fear of jail makes me no crook.
I do my writing and read a book.
Ambition failed me, by and large.
I made on the world no barrage.
Books I published by the score,
mostly out of print in any store.

What am I living for?
I love friendship and love,
but solitude is a must,
wherein I do my contemplation
and ponder the interrelation
of facts and factors in life's factory
which I find mostly satisfactory.

WHAT POETRY DOES AND DOESN'T.
IF YOU BUY THIS, IT'S CHEAPER BY THE DOZEN.

The poet resorts to tortuous rhymes
to make his bells sound like chimes.
He tries to get the right effect
though it comes out less than perfect.
He exaggerates every truth
to make modesty sound uncouth.
Poetry is like propaganda
to make the meager sound grander;
and thus resembles advertising
that makes the expected sound surprising.
This is my investigative finding.
The moral? Never trust rhyme
to sound like it means what it says,
but dupes you into a phony daze
to nightly light up ordinary days.
Poetry is a lightweight that artificially weighs,
thinking up extraordinary ways
to fool you with its unholy rays.
Maybe it's only an immature phase
along the road to greatness,
like making the hungry eat less,
yet over-eating to unruly excess

while filling the belly nevertheless
with imaginary food never consumed
but making the eater prematurely tombed.

EXIT OF SEX'S EX

Goodbye to sex accompanied by glamour
and all that arousing clamor.
I'm too old to have fun any more
with no more hankie-pankie in store.
Youth's been cut open to its core
and all the romance ripped out,
leaving me a wizened old man
limping along in slow tread.
Sleep is my only use for the bed.
Yet that's still preferable to being dead.
At the end of the day, all's said.
Do I leave with regret?
My bare reply is "You bet!"
said with dear little breath yet.
That's my final reply
to the bad news I'm about to die.
Hearing this, have a good cry.
You survived me. You're still high.
Only grant me our intimate sigh.

FEMALE DEATH EROTICS.
AN OLD WOMAN, HER TIME READY,
SEDUCES HER VULNERABLE DEATH.

Being older, I get bolder,
being a temptress of Death,

who now sniffs and winks at me,
aroused by increasing availability,
getting the hots for me
whose common wrinkled face
makes me more attractive to lusting Death
eager to tear away my departing breath.
Thus here I am, available.
He's never been failable,
favoring the fallible,
having had so many a victim.
All I have to do is sit and wait for him,
having done my tempting already,
so it seems like we're going steady.
Get me. I'm more than ready.

MY CREDO, HITHER TO AND FRO.

The nightmare faces me
that life is ebbing away.
I'm not religious, so I don't pray.
Beyond living and dying,
life has no meaning.
It's not meant to be anything specific.
I bear no cause or slogan about it
to focus my energy on
except just to get along.
The childhood I went through,
young manhood and middle age,
added to longevity I accumulated,
but what has it all illustrated?
For what was I ever "fated"?
To get my writing done and try to publish,

as a means of aiming at the public.
The public mainly turned its back
with massive indifference,
thus thwarting ambition,
which dies of attrition.
I've made a few contributions
locally here and there,
which slight markets could bare,
which I merely bear.
I loved loyally my baseball team,
whose win could make me scream
in silent inwardness.
I loved friendship and love,
mainly my dear wife's.
Now about to take leave,
I'll permanently "turn a new leaf,"
having lived life without belief.
Now I'm subject to others' grief
or else wide indifference
that makes no difference.

AS USUAL

Life and death are two basic poles
which I contemplate on my strolls
which lead me swiftly nowhere,
so back home I must repair
and look outward in a stare
or inward with calm gloom,
my regular life to resume.
So life as usual proceeds,
still wondering where it leads.

MY SUPERIOR RIVAL MAKES ANOTHER OMINOUS ARRIVAL, DOOMING MY ROMANTIC SURVIVAL.

My love and I had a kiss
to prove that nothing was amiss.
We were already engaged to marry.
To delay further was to tarry.
Suddenly she met my superior rival
who tore her away on his arrival,
thus dooming me to non-survival
in this bitter competition.
It was a repetition
of a previous loved one being taken;
and henceforth I was forsaken
when she fell for my superior rival
on his long-ago arrival.
He's my nemesis for sure,
and leaves me abandoned on the shore
by loved ones he's taken away
to ruin my perfectly planned day.
May he disappear, is what I pray.
But he's too much there in the flesh,
continuing to act unforgivably fresh
as a promiscuous lech.
His evil portrait I could etch,
after a vulgar preliminary sketch.

HEARTBREAK AND TRAGEDY.
LACK OF MONEY WOULDN'T CARRY ME,
SO RELUCTANTLY SHE COULDN'T MARRY ME.

I was financially deplorable,
so my dear adorable
had to marry a wealthier man
to get the children I couldn't afford.
I had to give her up with tears
after some few great years
in her true-love company.
But childbirth was on her clock,
so she said goodbye forever
and broke my proverbial heart
demolished by future babies' dart
that pierced me through and through
as she exited from my agonized view.
Money is a bitch bruiser
when its lack caused me to lose her.

A PLANNED FALL
TO SIGNAL "THAT'S ALL."

Life buckles under and gives to death
permission with full regret
to go ahead and wipe me out,
even plucking the snot from my snout
while all the rest of me goes south,
drooling a stream from my mouth.
My eyes close to my final scene,
eyeing the earth covered with green
to wish me a bliss of a farewell
before I break my bones down the stairwell,

which was an accident I actually planned,
deliberately disregarding where I land.
Life's sentence had no word to follow "and."

THE NEW YORK SCENE ON A CLOUDY BUSINESS DAY FROM THE MORNING'S POINT OF VIEW CONCERNING MORE THAN A FEW WHOSE FUTURES ARE DAILY DUE.

Skies and clouds had a conference:
Should we rain today on New York?
We've already been forecast to do so,
so predictability's odds favor us
to let go from tumultuous clouds
a torrent on the New York crowds
in the morning but then dry out
and watch the umbrellas vanish
from our imperial heights
while New Yorkers pursue their delights
or miserable failures.
It was a business day,
where salary earning will preside
over the variegated working tide
including the lunch hour break
where bargains are sought at eating shops
where business people make their stops.
Meanwhile, regulated traffic proceeds
in controlled directions,
and various young men conceal their erections
that concern their private lives.
Altogether, our industry thrives.
The business of living includes money.

Both genders think of their honey.
Love and indifference collide.
Enjoy the New York ride
or rather the walk
on the grimy New York sidewalk.

ELEGY TO JIMMY STAGNO.
WILL "YANKEES FOREVER" END? NO.

We thought they'd never end,
those old days, my friend.
Seventy years we knew each other
but no more, due to death
by you, since I'm writing this,
missing forever all that bliss
of regular continuity
in periodic regularity.
Now our life-death disparity
makes me your survivor,
but who's ever a reviver?
Being cut totally in half
makes incomplete all that combined laugh.
The laughs we had and considered thought
to what finality have been brought?
We compared the Major Leaguers
and quoted their averages,
went at them like calm savages.
It's an uninterrupted conversation
under the cover of subdued elation.

TRIBUTE TO FRED GUTZEIT
WHO GAVE THE ART WORLD AN EXTRA BITE
AND INTRODUCED COLORS INTO A NEW LIGHT.

Birth gave you a burgeoning start
to promote your venture into art
that started with an infantile crayon
and later gave you oils to play on
in developing a rectangular canvas
with swirls of colors and lines
made to your precise designs.
The whole canvas made a statement
that you somehow forged ahead
to stand the art world on its head
like the simple procedure of going to bed.
You were a natural artist
and from nature got an assist.
One flicker from your strenuous wrist
settled your future reputation
with an original impact on the world
which your inventions liberally unfurled
to meet the eye straight through
from inside the whole frame
and turn art into another game.
Hence rose the impulse of your fame.

[A video of Marvin's visit to his friend Fred's studio can be found on Vimeo and the transcript in Life's Tumultuous Party.*]*

TWO OVERLAPPINGS OF FRUITLESS GRAPPLINGS.

I who sought poetic fame
watched my pursuit pull up lame.
In consolation, I found a dame
poetically built, so I married her
so hastily, we didn't confer.
We found that we didn't prefer
each other, so quickly divorced
like my poems, which seemed forced.
Those twin failures smoothly crossed
like a lovely coincidence
of star-struck incidents.

AT HORST. WE LAUGHED HOARSE.

Lucky to be a party
by invitation to Horst's party,
we all were glad to flock
at his memorable loft
on Seventh Avenue, south of Penn Station,
for drinks and exceptional food
cooked by Horst from Germany,
who designed great clothing
costing money for an expert craftsman
whose precision of an exclusive draftsman
gave theatrical fashion a boost,
and in those days he ruled the roost.
I also had the privilege
of visiting him alone,
sitting across from his throne
for just jovial conversation for its own

between well-served drinks
and savory sausage too.
He preferred to laugh if he could
between throatsful of a German accent.
We laughed and laughed in philosophy,
making the world wiser between us.
Conversation word by word
painted the world sublimely absurd.
No one else was there for a third,
except beautiful queens of my rhymes:
Phyllis or Lynn came at other times
to combine ornament with intellect.
Horst had a great hand
of who to invite to his private land.
He conducted the occasion with his wand
for an atmosphere more than fond.

[Marvin wrote: "Horst really has only that one name for a name. He's retired, but was a clothes maker . . . for private fashion-minded clients. For 25 consecutive football super bowls, he in his working loft/residence gave eating & drinking parties for many lucky guests including me."]

MYRTLE'S TOPIC OF GENDER THEORY ABSORBED ME TILL I GOT WEARY.

I nestled in her arms,
a victim of her charms.
When she allowed me a kiss,
it was an invitation to bliss.
Her lips were hard to miss,
between her chin and nose.
Myrtle was my special gal,
too sexy for only a pal.

Into intimacy we soared
before sanity was restored.
It kept me from being bored.
Myrtle and I, thanks to evolution,
found a perfect solution
to problems of reproduction.
We made a big production
of separating each gender
from the other in tender
opposition to pull apart,
each drawn to the other,
yet feeling fully different.
The division of the sexes
not only perplexes,
it points out polarity
as a beneficial disparity.
We had a child, Myrtle
having conveniently rhymed with "fertile."

DISAPPEAR.
BUT THEY'RE SO DEAR.

To think of all the people I knew who are dead
makes me ready to be put to bed.
They overwhelm me with the difference
between them then and them now,
in their wretched condition
of having no position.
They're empty completely,
wiped out neatly.
I remember them as wonderful people
each in his or her own right.
Memories are trying to revive them.

How wonderful they were!
I'm overcome. What could I say?
Nothing. Let the memories jolt me
and still see they're not here
in their private worlds of disappear.

LOVING CANDACE WATT
AFTER WE'VE TIED THE KNOT
AND CONSTRUED OUR LIFE PATH PLOT.

Love for Candace Watt
is an act I'll never blot.
She supplies the "who" and "what,"
but only I supply the "why."
How my love to her does fly!
It holds up the whole sky
just to come winging by
to drop me off to see her.
What does it take to be her?
She controls her own essence.
Cork off, watch the effervescence!

THE PIGEON.
FOR ITS WELFARE, PITCH IN.

A pigeon's life is often misunderstood.
It's not a squirrel, but an actual bird
whose voice coo-coos when it's heard.
It seems to be puffed out pompous,
but humbly goes about its business
whether on ground, tree, or air
looking to live and breed and not despair.

It lives alongside humanity
and never utters profanity.
Though not looking too beautiful,
it goes about its business, duty-ful.
It shares the world with other species,
but sometimes on car-tops leaves its feces.

TO CANDACE WATT
WHO'S CONNECTED MY DOT
ALL OVER THE LOT.

By love we're attached,
so it's a mutual catch
to open the latch
for a suitable love match
punctuated by a kiss and hug
to catch the pesky love bug.
Candace Watt and I
are eye to eye together
tightly woven in a tether.
Come out and feel the weather.
We're an acceptable duo,
and our bloods' traffic will flow
any which way to stay
the way we are; at long last
we've built our love to last
through the lulls and through the blast.
For this ride we clutch fast.

OLD AGE'S DECLINE.
I LOST WHAT WAS MINE.
NO WONDER I WHINE.

Old age is threatening my trade
as a poet, making me forget words
that were apt, and substituting instead
weak words that mar my poem
by being inadequate to the subject.
Handicapped by old age,
I give up my old trade
and become a former poet.
Everyone will know it.
How I weep for former *poetry*.
As a past master, I now climb a *lower tree*.
The branch cracks and I fall free.
Fame has forgot my name
but elects me to the Hall of Shame.
Youth fled, I'm never the same,
even getting rejected by a dame
who was my primary erotic aim.

WHAT TO WRITE.
WILL IT HAVE BITE?
I'LL TRY, WITH ALL MY MIGHT.
LET INSPIRATION LIGHT.

I've run out of what to write about.
I've used up themes of birth and death,
also of human drama,
utilizing my good English grammar.
A new topic is what I need.
I'll think about it while I feed,

searching all about the human breed
and how we've arrived from evolution—
—there in fact is a good solution!
I'll roll my sleeves up and write
an essay in the form of poem.
If negative, the reader will groan.
The evolution part will be untechnical
due to my lack of knowledge:
There was no such course in college
when I illegally audited long ago.
Here I go, wish me luck.
For all my efforts, I'll never earn a buck.
I'm not well known,
so here I'll go, with a groan.
At least it will be my very own.
It'll praise the non-extinction
of our human breed that achieved distinction.

TO AL LEHMAN

Your mom squeezed you through the canal,
till there you are, Al,
squealing out your born birth
till later interred inside earth.
Meanwhile, what a life you had!
Sometimes good, sometimes bad.
You were quite a guy, Al.
You died first, my dear pal.
I'm your survivor, reluctantly,
till I also succumb
to equal you in mutually being dumb,
never knowing where the hell we came from.
It's hard to summarize the whole sum.

**BROKEN-UP FRIENDSHIP
BY DEATH'S BOLD STROKE
TO SEPARATE US FOLK.
AM I HERE? GIVE ME A POKE.
I RIVAL JIMMY STAGNO
IN COMIC COMPETITION
WORTHY OF ABSURD FICTION.**

Jimmy Stagno and I are severed
by death (his property)
that divided us drastically.
I'm still here, but not lastingly.
Jimmy's out of it altogether,
independent of "whether."
Severely broken is our tether,
parting death's silent dimension
from life's ongoing tension
belonging still to me,
breathing tenuously
from emphysema's sour lungs
that keep constipated my dungs.
Into such agony am I flung,
that Jimmy is almost better off.
But I envy him not,
even with bowels in a knot.
He can't even connect a dot.
I over-connect a lot.
Is it a deep-seated plot?
Are we in competition?
This is impossible friction,
belonging only to fiction.

A SOCIAL PARASITE,
I'M OFTEN NEAR FOOD'S GREEDY SIGHT,
GOOD FOR RECURRENT APPETITE
FOR A NICE FREE SNEAKY BITE.

Life is lonelier as I lose friends
to our mutual enemy, death,
with me remaining alive
lucky enough to survive
but not necessarily to thrive,
as the older I get
gives me too much to forget
and adds to what I regret.
Did I win or lose more in bet
considered in gross or in net?
I remember friends who can't requite,
having lost memory to death.
I'm still going strong.
In society's stronghold I belong,
being a popular "man about town"
in art gallery and book-launching receptions
free-loading with underhand deceptions,
helping myself to free food and red wine
so available, who am I to whine?
I gorge myself, so I don't have to dine,
but just sleep off my drunken bout
like a combined mooch and greedy lout.
Uninvited, sometimes I get thrown out
from where I try to crash,
hoping to compensate for my lack of cash.
Some day this way of living will go smash,
not till my bones grind to ash.

HELPLESS IN MY PREDICAMENT. ACCEPTING IT AND GIVING UP ARE MY ONLY RECOURSES.

Remembering dead old friends
is my only refuge
against having no contact whatever.
These are one-sided "relationships."
I remember them.
They don't remember me.
Should I chafe, being helplessly unrequited?
We sure aren't united.
I'm lonely. They're nothing.
It's an inconsolable distance.
I give no resistance,
except increasing memory
against the invisible enemy.
What can I do
in these lop-sided circumstances?
Do voodoo dances?

WHERE DID THEY GO?

Old friends died,
but it wasn't deliberate
to make me feel alone and deprived.
They were too involved in dying
to likely consider me,
being so preoccupied
with dying's awful self-ness
as the highest priority
in their self-drama.
Where did they go? Alabama?

THE HORRIBLE COMPARING,
BEYOND MORTAL DARING.

My best former friends are all dead,
so what do I make of them instead
of having them within hailing distance
to Email or phone up?
The puzzling distinction between them and me
is the question, "What does it mean to be?"
Did I one-up them by still being alive?
Am I gloating that I survive?
Do I think, "Better them than me
to have surrendered life's meaning,
since there's no in-betweening?"
Either you're dead or not.
My dead best friends I miss.
Why them than me?
To say I'm "better off"
is boastful with relief.
I retain positive belief.
I'm conscious and mortal.
Where they "are" is awful.

VOWING NEVER TO FORGET.
STILL, IT ALREADY HAPPENED YET.

How can I possibly part from my beloved?
I will never have recovered
from the last sight I had of her,
before all the rest became a blur
with tears rolling from each eye,
teaching me how to die
following the catharsis of my cry.

Yet soon memory will fly
from that touching scene of goodbye.
Together we would lie
and vow never to forget.
Still, recently – would you have bet?
The mind lapsed with total neglect,
and we blundered into our defect
which only time maybe would correct,
to bring back remembrance
of our imperishable romance
that happened once in a chance.
The mind has paused in its dance.

THE BOND'S FATE
WITH YOUR DEAR MATE.

When two lives join each other
in friendship or in love,
the bond they share
is always there,
being enacted or resting.
While one expresses,
the other is expressed to,
happy to receive.
Then they reverse their turns.
Fair is fair.
How reliable!
The bond strengthens
as it lengthens.
Let nothing interfere
with this double near-and-dear
of inclusive enclosure
with or without disclosure.

Sometimes it gets lost, I fear,
never to return.
It's nobody's turn.

MASSIVE DISAGREEMENT, DOGMATICALLY VEHEMENT.

Billions of people believe they'll get to "heaven,"
so as to feel better about dying.
If I protest, they'll say I'm lying.
They can't prove their point, I can't mine.
So we're at an impasse.
Well, let that pass.
But neither of us can, alas,
and almost come to grips,
hoping the opposition flips.

BEING AN EGOMANIAC SHOWS YOU DEVOID OF ANY LACK. YOU'RE SUPERIOR AT OTHERS' EXPENSE. IN THE RATIO OF THINGS, THAT MAKES SENSE.

Make sure you prioritize
yourself as number one,
cutting others down to size,
even including their demise.
You come first, remember that.
Memorize this credo
so you know where to go
without getting vertigo.
Others are human, just like you.
Consider them in a more minor view

in relative rank of importance.
Is this too snobbish a stance?
Yourself is whom you must enhance
at the pompous head of the dance,
majestic leader of circumstance.
Let others go to relative hell.
Cast on them your imperious spell.
Should they protest, quell
their minor revolt
with an electronic jolt.
If they chase you, bolt.

RHODA.
EARLY ON WE SHARED A SODA.
THEN IN YOUTH I RODE HER.

Rhoda was sexy, so I rode her
till sex wore out,
and we mutually married apart,
each with a separate partner
in a separate apartment.
But memory has a compartment.
I remembered Rhoda all throughout
our later lives apart.
I didn't put it behind me.
But don't remind me.
I contacted her by Email
as my favorite old female.
What's the ending to this tale?
She never replied, so I phoned her.
She cordially replied,
but romance had died.
Sentiment had applied,

but Rhoda gave it rejection.
That was our last connection.
Goodbye to Rhoda, my former mate,
having nothing further to state.
Love dies, and sometimes late.

HE DIED.
YOU'RE DENIED.

Don't expect your dead friend to requite
the way you remember him quite.
He's in no condition to do so.
Don't feel betrayed by his neglect.
Neglect is all he's capable of.
Consider his circumstances.
Death confers passivity on him,
which he's helpless to resist.
Your friendship is now one-sided.
Your end is manned fully.
He doesn't keep up his end,
but can you fault him?
If you wish his death would go away
and be replaced by life's revival,
you're "barking up the wrong tree."
Accept his death realistically.
If you have sentimental tears,
shed them, don't hold back.
You're on the right track.
You're keeping friendship alive
in proud handicap's only choice.
Fond memory needs not rejoice.

A SUDDEN REVERSAL FROM DESPAIR TO JOY. IS THIS A REHEARSAL FOR SWEET INNOCENCE AS A BOY?

I must stop wanting what I can't get
and be saddled with regret
that gives me a sour outlook
of pessimism wherever I look.
Failure haunts me with every desire
till I feel: "Why not expire?
Life is a place of non-fulfillment
leading to bodily illment.
What's the use of going on?
My post-death skeleton I'll don.
This is enough to brood upon.
My carefree youth is completely gone,
to be replaced by a morbid death thought.
Mathematically, my life sums up as naught.
Where's the wonderful life I had sought?
It was a dream that never came true.
Dark grim gloom is my only view."
But now happiness returns.
My paper-thin pessimism burns
to an ash I throw away.
I gladly resume my youthful play,
and merriment rules my entire day.
What accounts for this abrupt change
to give my emotions such range?
It came out of the invisible air
to render a knock-out blow to despair.

WHO AM I HAUNTED BY?
I'LL NEVER FIND OUT, BY AND BY.

Uneasy dreams haunt me at night,
paranoia by day.
I'm a mess. People make me nervous
without any provocation.
I can't put myself together
into an orderly procedure.
I'm even disturbed at my leisure.
Does the world contain a solution?
No. I'm a marked man.
Mysterious voices invade my head
whose messages are indecipherable.
My vision is rocked by jagged edges
swooped suddenly out of the void.
I squirm but can't avoid
this unprofitable activity
that I'm a puppet to.
Who's masterminding me?
Who has a hold of my psychee?
Who's billed me for a fee?
Some ghost with a foreign language
who puts me under the claw of anguish,
that scratches me to an intolerable itch.
Who's the culprit? Some indeterminate bitch
whose former guise was a witch.
Someone I knew? But which?

TRYING TO MARRY RUTH.
BUT SHE PUT MONEY IN THE WAY
LIKE A VIOLENT BIRD OF PREY.

I wanted to marry Ruth
but had yet to propose.
I thought up a good line
to make my proposal seem benign
and not too threatening.
Ruth deliberated, then accepted,
provided I displayed my bank account
and financial records.
I thought this was a mercenary attempt
as a gold-digger just proposed to,
and told her so, vehemently.
She asked me, in ruthless terms,
"How much are you worth? I won't marry you
unless you own enough account
to the certified right amount."
I said this was totally unromantic
and deliberately calculating.
Our marriage is still waiting.
That was thirty years ago.
I'm a lonely bachelor, all alone,
reduced to a bare-bone
existence as a poor man
with a lower-wage job.
What a bad job wooing Ruth!
It never got to the point of truth.
She's married with four children,
in middle class circumstances.
I'm lost with a lack of money,
with no one to call "my honey."
I'm frightened by old age,

qualified to be a sage.
Inside, I'm all in a rage.

ONLY WANT WHAT YOU CAN GET

Be careful of what you want,
because you may not get it,
and would have to regret it.
To avoid that catastrophe,
be ready to pay your fee
for frustration-prevention,
which is my new invention:
Only want what you can get.
That eliminates the losing bet.
Make sure you're very well met
with the right odds in your favor.
Must you then adopt Christ as your savior?
No. The religious angle won't pay off
because heaven doesn't exist,
though clergymen do persist,
and put salvation high on their list.
If you say nay, raise your fist.

A VISITATION.
WAS IT A CREATION?
OR A PREMONITION
FROM THE DEEPS OF INTUITION,
OR THE CUNNING OF VOLITION?
WHAT WAS MY EXACT POSITION?

I met my loved one all of a sudden
like the snapping of a button

that came loose from a surprised shirt.
She wore a lovely skirt
and a blouse on top.
My eyes went "pop!"
to meet my love on the spot.
I couldn't quite connect the dot.
So I'd just leave it at that
and returned to sleep,
leaving my mind to explore the deep.
Was it a dream or not?
Or maybe a forecast?
It was only a small blast.
Its effects would not last.
After rising, I pondered again
and wondered if ever when
this vision would so recur,
as to clarify its partial blur.
From it, what would I infer?
There was no point of desperation.
The issue unscrewed itself and went loose.
Was I a hermit or recluse?
I went to a party and all of a sudden
I saw her alive like a popping button
with the threads dangling loose.
"Are you the same one?" I asked.
In each other we soon basked.

WOOING JANE.
LATER I WOULD COMPLAIN.

I was attracted to Jane
and considered marriage,
though too shy to propose,

for being unwilling to impose.
Yet I had to take a stand,
to vindicate myself as a man.
So I took my heart in my mouth
and uttered these words:
"Jane, since I love you
and you seem fond of me,
let's get hooked to each other
with emphasis on married love.
I vow to treasure you
and fulfill your whole life."
She took this calmly
but didn't want to harm me.
"I'm engaged to another," she replied,
"but thanks for the compliment.
I know your proposal was well meant.
I would have obliged, to the extent
of volunteering an exuberant 'yes.'
However, my fiancee would protest.
I'm quite fond of you, nevertheless.
Should he ever regret marriage to me,
that would liberate me. Rejoice.
You're at least my second choice."
I fainted at the sound of her voice.
But her marriage turned out complete,
and I couldn't compete.
Jane was lost forever.
I recovered soon, however,
and landed on my feet.
Down the line, my life took a new turn
with a new woman to woo and earn.
No wrath entered my soul to burn.

DOLORES WAS FOR US.

So never to bore us,
Dolores was for us
getting married,
so we never tarried,
but did it quick
like a jumping candlestick
before the advent of Edison
who put a lightbulb in his medicine
the better to be cured of darkness
that clad our nudity in starkness.
Dolores was my graceful bride.
She devoured her breakfast and me beside.
All was light between me and her.
Whatever I suggested, she'd concur
without even the need to confer.
Our engine buzzed like a whir.
That's only the way we were.
But later in life she died.
Her memory fills my pride.

MY URGENT ACQUAINTANCE WAS IN AN AWFUL HURRY. I WISH HIM WELL. SHOULD I WORRY?

Life can be a bundle of fun,
but don't take it too lightly.
In reality, life is earnest,
and favors the firmest
in taking life seriously.
"Seriously, if I wasn't so busy,

you and I could have a meal together.
But right now, you'd be surprised
how time and the years fly by.
Speaking of that, I've got to fly.
It's important I meet this guy.
He offers me a partnership,
and I'm tempted to take it.
I'll hurry now, so I can make it.
Take care, and regards to your wife.
If we can get together, you bet your life
I'll call you up soon.
It's been many a moon.
Goodbye, take care,
and don't forget to do your share
in contributing to my Cause.
Why? Just because.
I'm so busy, I can't pause."
Then he leaves me in a flash,
shouting on route, "Sorry, I must dash."
If he takes a car in his haste,
I hope it won't crash and his life waste.

ELEGY TO THE BEST FRIEND

The death of Jimmy Stagno hit me hard.
I'm still waiting for his car to pick me up
at the Long Island train station
to go through our conversational rituals
and play pool at the Senior Center
and eat at our restaurant.
I knew him seventy three years
starting early adolescent
at Junior High School

near Bay Parkway and Kings Highway.
We took long walks to Coney Island.
We played versions of beloved baseball.
We weighed the Yankees' chances.
Our families were both poor.
You left High School and became a die maker
and father of five.
We were born a month apart.
Our wives got to know each other.
The train station no longer expects.
Our friendship is now one-sided.
You were there. Where are you?
I can still "see" you
almost ready to respond
to my well-prepared wit
to bring you to a fit.

IN THE NIGHT

Fallen upon unlistening ears,
my "I love you" gets nowhere.
She's asleep, that's why.
Respect her sleeping spell
and her unheard dream. Is all well?
She moves barely a fraction.
I'm ignorant of her dream's action.
Am I the subject of it?
If so, how I love it!
Or am I her nightmare?
I didn't mean to give her a scare.
Upon awakening, we'll be a pair.
Meanwhile, I gently stare.

SAD RHYMES OF TIME'S CRIMES.

Memories are the source of woe
that the joys of long ago
are today barred to you.
Today is false, yesterday is true
lodged in memory's case.
You're only granted a bitter trace
of yesterday's retracted gift.
Its splendors are today's meager thrift.
Youth was better able to take them.
Old age's memory can merely fake them.
That good old past
haunts us with its merry blast.
It taunts you, having gone too fast.
"Here today, gone tomorrow"
is your sure guide to current sorrow.
Thus past and present compared
show how downward we have fared.
May further severance be spared.

HOW TO PUT EVERYTHING IN A POEM, WHICH THE CRITICS ARE BOUND TO CONDONE AND WHISTLE TO THE TUNE ON THE WAY HOME.

Do poems need to rhyme?
It's considered no crime
to let stanzas end blank.
We have free verse to thank
that prose is a respected vehicle,
and too much rhyme is mere treacle.
Prose has a journalistic reputation;

But stick it in a poetic situation
to perform a variety act
till nothing—absolutely nothing—is lacked.
Comfort every taste with delicate tact.
Combine imaginary fantasy with fact.

[Maggie asked: "What about rhythm?"
Marvin replied: "I forgot rhythm, & too late now. Rhythm didn't make the cut, but it needn't feel ashamed of itself & thereby develop an inferiority complex. I'll do it double justice some time in belated compensation. I swear, by my word of honor. Its neglect will be redeemed."]

AFTERWORD: A MINI MEMOIR OF MARVIN
by Deborah Sanderson and Peter Jackson

Deborah first encountered Marvin at a party in London circa 1972 when she found herself sitting next to him on a sofa in an elegant Kensington drawing room. Since then he has been a unique planet in our social solar system. In the old days, his orbit brought him here every summer, when he would spend several weeks in possession of whichever of his friends' mansions happened to be vacant. He had a wide choice of hospitable but absent hosts, and it was thin pickings if he ever had to apply to us. Which was fortunate as our home could not have survived a repetition of the time he put the electric kettle, still plugged in, on the gas stove. Once installed, Marvin planned his summer campaigns, taking in baseball in the park and enthusiastic games of cricket in the counties. But most of all, he worked out who he wanted to see and which parties he wanted to attend or, failing an invitation, to crash. Marvin approaches parties with the utmost seriousness. As he has been half deaf since early childhood, you would think that noisy crowds would be a deterrent, but instead they create the conditions for the exclusive one-to-one conversations that are his speciality. These would begin at the party and continue with the inevitable post-mortem phone call the next morning, when the event would be anatomised with gusto until, like the carcass of a chicken, it was picked bare.

It's some time since Marvin came to London, and our occasional trips to NYC are no substitute for his annual pilgrimages. On the other hand, there isn't a day when we don't think of him because there isn't a day without the arrival of at least one fresh conversation or versification in our email inbox. They're no substitute for a face-to-face with Marvin, but they're the next best thing. The verses' manic rhymes bear witness to his weakness for appalling puns, while the conversations are quite simply a dialectical method of his own invention. The very word conversation includes both verse and converse and the format perfectly captures his devotion to the art of communication. If Marvin can't have a conversation with someone else, he'll have one with himself. Long may he enlighten us about birth, youth, friendship, love, sex, old age, death and art. As he says *"It's extraordinary how much life excites."*

November 2020

ABOUT THE AUTHOR

Marvin Cohen (born Brooklyn, July 6, 1931), is the author of four episodic novels, a collection of plays, two volumes of verse, a book on baseball, and several collections of shorter pieces—stories, dialogues, parables, and idiosyncratic essays. His work has also appeared in more than 100 publications, from the experimental to the mainstream, including: *Ambit, Antaeus, Assembling* ("a collection of otherwise unpublishable writings"), the *Beat Scene* (alongside Kerouac, Ginsberg and Corso), *Chelsea, Fiction, The Hudson Review,* Thomas Merton's *Monks Pond, New Directions in Prose and Poetry, The Transatlantic Review, The New York Times, Harper's Bazaar* and *Vogue*.

His 1980 play *The Don Juan and the Non-Don Juan* was first performed at the New York Shakespeare Festival as part of the Poets at the Public Series; staged readings have featured Richard Dreyfuss, Wallace Shawn, Jill Eikenberry and Mimi Kennedy.

Cohen was born in Brooklyn, New York City. He has described himself as one who has "risen from lower-class background to lower-class foreground." He studied art at Cooper Union but left college to focus on writing. He supported himself with a series of short-term jobs including mink farmer and merchant seaman. He later taught creative writing at various New York colleges including the New School, the City College of New York, C.W. Post of Long Island University, and Adelphi University. He is married and currently lives with his wife in Manhattan.

www.ingramcontent.com/pod-product-compliance
Lightning Source LLC
Chambersburg PA
CBHW011139290426
44108CB00020B/2683